MW00849490

Praise for *Letters on Liturgy*

"Nothing is more important than liturgy, the source and summit of the life of the Church, and nothing seems more fragile—which makes Fr. Dwight's book a refreshing, inspiring read. Miles away from destructive polemics and dry erudition, it provides an opportune, accessible catechesis such as should accompany any effort to promote better understanding and practice of the services of the Church. Here we find good advice, good taste, joyful patience, and realistic hope. A powerful little book on a most important subject."—DOM XAVIER PERRIN, OSB, Abbot of Quarr Abbey, Isle of Wight

"With a vitality of style matching his theological ambition to re-enchant Catholic worship, Dwight Longenecker educates, instructs, and inspires. This is a book that helps both priests and lay Catholics enter more fully into the celebration of the Mass."—R. R. RENO, Editor, *First Things*

"In *Letters on Liturgy*, Fr. Dwight Longenecker boldly calls for Catholic liturgy to be 're-enchanted' with beauty, reverence, and grace. He demonstrates a profound grasp of the difficulties often found in contemporary Catholic worship while reminding readers that through faith, hope, and action we may reclaim our glorious heritage. The writing is practical, deep, witty, and persuasive. It is a rare and welcome fusion of profound love of the liturgy

and deep compassion for the faithful. Thanks be to God!"
—W. WINSTON ELLIOTT III, Publisher of the *Saint Austin Review* and *The Imaginative Conservative*

"I highly recommend *Letters on Liturgy*. It is a thoughtful reflection on the nature and purpose of the Sacred Liturgy. Fr. Longenecker charitably corrects modern errors, excesses, and distortions, while offering also practical advice on how to restore greater reverence and recover lost traditions. It is perfect for seminarians and clergy of every rank or age. The laity too will benefit from this superb book and be better equipped to work with their clergy for a more excellent celebration and experience of the Sacred Liturgy."—REV. MSGR CHARLES POPE, *Pastor* of Holy Comforter St. Cyprian Catholic Church

"*Letters on Liturgy* is a deeply enjoyable dive into what liturgy does that nothing else can: enact what it signifies. Fr. Longenecker persuasively shows us that to re-enchant the liturgy is to re-enchant the world, and thereby make our ancient Faith new."—MAGGIE GALLAGHER, Executive Director, Benedict XVI Institute

"The point of beauty is the truth: nothing more and nothing less—which is why liturgy matters. In *Letters on Liturgy*, Fr. Dwight Longenecker reminds us that beautiful liturgy brings us ever closer to ultimate realities, at the heart of which is the Logos Himself, who brings us eternal life."—SAMUEL GREGG, Acton Institute

Letters on Liturgy

LETTERS

on

LITURGY

⊕

Fr Dwight Longenecker

Foreword by
Archbishop Salvatore Cordileone

 Angelico Press

First published
by Angelico Press 2020
© Fr Dwight Longenecker 2020
Foreword © Archbishop Salvatore Cordileone 2020

All rights reserved

No part of this book may be reproduced or transmitted,
in any form or by any means, without permission.

For information, address:
Angelico Press
4709 Briar Knoll Dr.
Kettering, OH 45429
angelicopress.com

978-1-62138-512-7 (pbk)
978-1-62138-513-4 (cloth)
978-1-62138-514-1 (ebook)

Cover design: Michael Schrauzer

CONTENTS

"If the Church is to continue to transform and humanize the world, how can she dispense with beauty in her liturgies, that beauty which is so closely linked with love and with the radiance of the Resurrection?"

—Pope Benedict XVI

Foreword

Archbishop Salvatore Cordileone

The only really effective apologia for Christianity comes down to two arguments, namely, the saints the Church has produced and the art which has grown in her womb.
— Pope Benedict XVI

T HE TRANSITION from seminary life to parish ministry as a newly ordained priest is always a tricky one to navigate. Despite an enhanced focus on pastoral formation in seminaries over the past few decades, the challenge will always remain of putting theory into practice. Just as it is impossible for a man and a woman to practice by trial and error what it is like to have a lifelong commitment of exclusive fidelity and openness to life but must instead develop the virtue necessary to maintain that commitment and then commit to it in marriage, so it is impossible for a young man to rehearse being an *alter Christus* for his people but must instead take all he has received in his seminary formation and live that out with Christian virtue and priestly spirituality.

Fr. Dwight Longenecker's most recent work, *Letters on Liturgy*, provides an invaluable tool to seminarians to help them make this historical passage in their lives. Written in a conversational style to Michael, a theoretical but easy-to-envision typical young man aspiring to give his life to God and the Church during his preparation for priestly ordination, all areas touching on Catholic worship are covered succinctly, practically, and with deep insight: music, art, and architecture; words and ritual; language and symbol; time and space; theology and pastoral practice; priestly identity and the mission and place of the Church vis-à-vis the post-modern world.

Fr. Longenecker draws masterfully on his broad background in literature and drama coupled with his own priestly formation and ample pastoral experience, all enhanced by his spiritual journey from Evangelicalism to Anglicanism and finally to the Catholic Church, to provide this bridge to a young man venturing forth from the seminary into a brave new world, a world which has not left the Church herself unaffected.

These are historically critical times for the Church, a time of crisis in the literal sense: a decisive point at which change must come, for better or for worse. Priests are the ones who most bear the brunt of this crisis, for they are the ones entrusted with proclaiming the timeless truth of the Gospel in the midst of the people whom they are called to love and serve but who live immersed in the hyper-secularized and socially deconstructed culture of our present-day society. Our young priests and seminarians never cease to inspire me as they step into this breach: they see the world for what it is, and understand how drastically different and more challenging it is from the one that their predecessors stepped into at the time of their ordination.

Still, even with such cognitive recognition, reality at

times strikes hard. Personal and pastoral failures do happen; disappointments are unavoidable and poor judgments are sometimes made. This present work can serve as a sort of pastoral reference book for all priests to fall back on at such moments in their life, a sort of vademecum for charting out and fulfilling a sound strategy of spiritual and ecclesial renewal for the people entrusted to the priest's pastoral care.

Letters on Liturgy, though, has something to offer all Catholics who truly love the Church and her heritage, and seek her renewed vitality at a time when it is needed the most. These *Letters* demonstrate how this heritage of timeless truth, beauty, and goodness is just as effective today as in any age, and can be realized in a way that is also sensitive and responsive to the times in which we live. The words of Pope Benedict XVI cited above provide the overall guiding principle, and indeed the very purpose of the Church, that perhaps has gotten lost in the wake of the social revolutions of the last fifty years (and more): God has entrusted this beautiful, powerful heritage to the Church in order to produce saints.

In one of his *Letters*, Fr. Longenecker puts this same insight in another way: "I believe the historic Catholic Faith offers the antidote to the candied poison of each passing age." He rightly places emphasis on the non-verbal ways in which this historic Faith is transmitted, and in particular, through beauty. His treatment of this is an especially valuable and urgently-needed aspect of this book, for in a hurting and divided world we need to re-appropriate the power of beauty to unite and heal. It is a power that is universal, and immediately recognizable. Practical experience bears this out.

Fr. Longenecker shares an example of his own in the building of his new parish church, where he observes that everyone who steps foot into the church—religiously minded or not, well-schooled in church life or not, professional or working-class—all have the same reaction: they are reduced to silence and utter, in a hushed tone, "it's beautiful." That is the non-verbal, intuitive power of beauty: it ennobles the soul and elicits an instinctive, spontaneous response that recognizes something of the presence of the sacred.

In addition to uniting, though, beauty also has a power to heal. Teaching sex-trafficked women to sing ancient Latin hymns to the Blessed Virgin Mary and forming a Gregorian chant schola for inmates detained in prison are two examples that come immediately to my mind. But one particularly poignant experience of my own came last year on All Soul's Day, when I celebrated the Duarte Lobo Solemn Requiem Mass at St. Mary's Cathedral in San Francisco with a world-class conductor and professional choir, sponsored by the Benedict XVI Institute for Sacred Music and Divine Worship. At the reception afterwards, a woman I'd never met before approached me to tell me what this Mass meant to her: "I've lost family members to communism. Their bodies were never recovered. It's been very painful and healing has been hard to reach. Today, in praying this Mass, I felt the peace of God at last."

Letters on Liturgy is as theologically sound and deeply insightful as it is easy to read and practical. It will, I am convinced, prove to be immensely helpful to all those who seek a renewal of sacred beauty and reverence in Church life, whether they are more traditionally-oriented in their liturgical preferences or find a more contemporary expression of beauty and reverence spiritually enriching. That, in and of itself, provides a force for unity in the Church. Yet another reason why *Letters on Liturgy* comes on the scene at just the right time.

This work is nothing less than a practical resource for priests to realize in their life and ministry the *apologia* for Christianity that a defiant world truly needs and unconsciously yearns for: the production of art from the Church's womb that mediates the presence of the sacred, and the witness of saints who personalize the power of the truth, beauty, and goodness of the transcendent majesty of God.

Introduction

I USED TO STUDY theology and philosophy. I enjoyed digging into books with long footnotes, German quotes, and bulging bibliographies. I read books that discussed in ever-so-serious tones the theories, histories, and ideologies of the liturgy.

Now, being older, much lazier, and not much wiser, I find such books tedious. Much of what I read seems to have been written before by better writers more succinctly. I grow impatient with all the references to boost arguments that are only read by people who already agree with them. It seems to me the authors are overthinking the problems and coming up with merely theoretical solutions. Remembering the doltish emperor in *Amadeus* who, when asked what he thought of Mozart's latest opera, pondered for a moment and said, "It has too many notes," in reading these books I sigh and say, "They have too many words."

But then I go right ahead and produce another such book, theorizing about the liturgy and doing some amateurish theological and psychological speculation. I admit it: I am a dilettante. I am the theological equivalent of the poetaster or the Sunday afternoon painter. It is very possible that I have written a book of balderdash which also has too many words. On the other hand, as a priest friend has said, "The liturgy is too important to be left to experts!"

In an attempt to make the book less tedious and more

accessible and practical, my thoughts are set out using the epistolary style. They are posed as letters to a seminarian named Michael. "Michael" is no one in particular, and the letters are not really letters.

I offer these thoughts on the liturgy as a parish priest and someone who has come into this maddening and glorious calling of Catholic priesthood from the world of speech, drama and English literature. I'm interested in how language works, the dynamic of drama and the chemistry of emotions. I'm fascinated by the hero's quest, the idea of catharsis in literature and how our emotions both constrain us and inspire. I like Joseph Campbell's *Hero with a Thousand Faces* and Bruno Bettleheim's *The Uses of Enchantment* and ponder how the alchemy of myths and fairy tales enlightens the sacred Scriptures and informs the mysterious exchange that takes place in the liturgy.

Speaking of enchantment, it is a sad truth that we live in the most disenchanted era of human history. Our utilitarian, techno-scientific world is obsessed with being useful. We have no room for magic, no time for the mysterious, the metaphysical, or the mystical. All of our angels have fallen—being fired down from full flight with a fusillade of facts. We are told that the sacraments are no more than symbols, that demons are merely the projection of our immature, terrified minds, and that all things mystical have turned out to be figments of a diseased imagination. What our ancestors thought was supernatural we are told is no more than a blip in the brain, a chemical reaction in the cerebellum, or a bad dream caused by an excess of pickled herring.

Our present state of mind is the result of half a millennium of increasingly wooden thought. From the nominalists onward, each succeeding generation was less imaginative and more literal. Each generation of thinkers took apart the supernatural world like the foolish boy who took apart the alarm clock looking for time. Bit by bit they dismantled the mythological, dissected the dogmas, and dismissed the miracles. They forgot Gandalf's dictum that "he who takes something apart to understand what it means departs from the path of wisdom." The result is our brave new world which is rational, hygienic, efficient and economical... and exceedingly dull.

We became disenchanted while at the same time longing for a greater meaning to life. Modern man is searching for his soul, but the Catholic Church, the one religion which still maintained the mystery of cultic worship and an unsettling system of sacrifice, dumbed itself down into a suburban therapy session, with a happy meal thrown in.

The one religion that acknowledged the need for cosmic redemption and the majesty of divine worship—the one religion that believed in sin, the fearsome possibility of hell, and the poignant hope of heaven threw out all that "Blood of the Lamb" malarkey in favor of psychotherapy. The one ancient religion which prayed for the dead, promoted apparitions of the Blessed Mother, believed in miracles, and stressed the need for supernatural salvation effectively threw all of that out in the revolution of the 1960s as fast you could say, "All We Are Saying is Give

Peace a Chance."

The one religion that ministered to peasants and princes, celebrated as saints both a dullard like Joseph Cupertino and the brilliant Thomas Aquinas, could both allow garish kitsch and embrace the glories of the Gothic, revel in the history of Rome and die in the dungeons of the gulag, produce little saints like Thérèse and astounding heroes like Isaac Jogues—this amazing, curious, unpredictable, subversive, and supernatural church became ho-hum. It became useful and socially relevant and about as interesting as the country club, the Rotary club, or the local library.

In other words, Catholics became disenchanted, and I use the word in both senses. Catholics became disenchanted with their church because their church had become disenchanted. In other words, they became disappointed and cynical because their once-glorious liturgy had become a blend of a pep rally and bland entertainment, with Father Fabulous presiding at Mass like an aging game show host endlessly trying to crank up enthusiasm for what was behind door number three. Buildings that were designed as beautiful and awesome temples of the Almighty were turned into community centers. New church buildings looked like a blend of parking garage and circus tent while the music of the revolution resembled a cross between activist folk ballads and campfire songs.

Horror of horrors, the Catholic Church had become useful! What a concept! Making the Church useful and relevant is rather like trying to turn *La Bohème* into a political statement against the low wages of artists and poets. Making the liturgy useful is like writing poetry as Marxist propaganda or regarding tap dancing as a method for losing weight.

The liturgy, like a fairy-tale play, is not meant to be merely useful. It is meant to be enchanting... and that is why we use chant. In a way, it is useful as a bridge is useful. It takes us across a great divide. The church is Bethel—the threshold of heaven—and in the liturgy we participate in the reality of heaven. The liturgy, if you like, is the practical way our society may be re-enchanted. It is a method beyond argument or debate because, like the Mona Lisa, Michelangelo's *Pieta*, or *The Marriage of Figaro*, it simply is.

The liturgy, rightly celebrated, brings millions of ordinary people into not a twilight zone, but a daybreak zone where they do not argue, explicate, or explain; they experience and participate in a conversation with the divine through the wonder of this unique enterprise we call worship.

And although I say our world is disenchanted, is it really? The pompous professors and media monsters would have us think so, but I am a parish priest. I work with children and adults who are ordinary people of simple faith. I am not so sure they are disenchanted, nor am I convinced that they disbelieve in the supernatural, dismiss myth, or scrutinize the faith with science. To be sure, in society at large traditional religion is in decline, but is faith in decline? I'm not convinced.

I do not see crowds of ordinary folks locked in existentialist intellectual anguish or some Nietzschean nightmare. Instead I find many who wholeheartedly believe the truths of the Faith. They do so with a rock-solid certainty spiced with a sweet inquisitiveness. They are curious and reverent, optimistic and trusting. These are not the mentally deficient, the inadequate, or the neurotic. They are solid and plain men, women, and children who live lives full of joy and sorrow, fear and hope. I like them very much.

Furthermore, I do not believe the power of fairy tales and myths is dead in our society. In fact, through superhero movies, science fiction tales, and fantasy sagas, myth and fairy tales are more potent in the popular imagination than ever before. Furthermore, interest in the preternatural, the unexplained, and the otherworldly is as high in the popular mind as ever before. It is the modernist clergyman who is embarrassed to discuss such things, and it is the postmodern professors looking down their noses at *hoi polloi* who are out of touch and out in the cold.

Therefore, I am optimistic about the re-enchantment of the liturgy, and the re-enchantment of the world through liturgy. People speak of the "reform of the reform." This is a polite way of saying that the half-baked experiment of modernism in the Catholic Church has been an obvious failure and needs to be overhauled. Let us not talk of "reform" but of renewal—the renewal of that which is ever ancient and ever new.

The traditional celebration of the Mass is transcendent, not trendy. It is transcendent not only because it connects us with the other realm, but also because it transcends particular cultures, time periods, ethnicities, and fashions. Gregorian chant is older than all of us, but ever-fresh. The liturgy with its constant echo of the Passion and Resurrection of the Lord Jesus is older in its archetypal symbolism and drama than the sagas of the Hebrews, the demigods of Delphi, and the horrific pyramids of the Aztecs. Through the liturgy we connect with all that is ancient about humanity's religious quest. Through the liturgy we send a bucket flying down into the deepest wells of history and the human heart to wheel up from the darkness the freshest of water.

I hope the notes that follow may help in the work of raising and releasing that water, for through it not only is our thirst refreshed, but we are born again.

Fr Dwight Longenecker
July 11, 2018
The Feast of St Benedict

1

First Thoughts

DEAR MICHAEL,

I enjoyed our conversation the other night about churchy stuff and your studies at seminary. So many people are pessimistic about the Church today. I'm not, and you and your fellow seminarians are a cause of encouragement. I'm glad you and the other guys seem interested in a more traditional style of liturgy. I'm convinced that the future of Catholicism is both up-to-date and rooted in the great traditions of the past.

It concerned me when you said how limited your seminary curriculum was in the areas of art, music, architecture, and iconography. I realize you need to do a lot of theology and philosophy, canon law and moral theology, but your training should also equip you for the tasks ahead. One day you guys are going to be in charge of building new churches and renovating old ones. There's also a lot to learn about sacred music and the practical points of celebrating the liturgy in an ordinary American parish.

I have to tell you straight-up that I am not a liturgical expert. I haven't studied the ancient forms and formulas or the history of the liturgy in much depth. I'm not a Latin or Greek scholar, and I know next to nothing about the various permutations of liturgical detail. I'm glad there are scholars like that out there, but I'm not one of them. To be honest, I go all fuzzy when the experts start talking about the East Syrian Rite of Addai and Mari, Alcuin's *antiphonarium missae*, or the development of the *camelaucum*.

What I know about the liturgy I picked up from basic understanding of Church documents, the *General Instruction of the Roman Missal*, the odd liturgy course, a few classic textbooks, and my life first as an Anglican priest and then as a Catholic. In other words, I am neither an expert nor a purist. My approach is to "say the black and do the red"—in other words, to celebrate the liturgy with simplicity and dignity according to the book.

However, there is more to celebrating Mass than just "saying the black and doing the red." What motivates me is the deeper meaning of worship. What are we doing and why are we doing it? I have already admitted that I am not a liturgist. I have to admit that I am also not a theologian. Great books have been written about the meaning of the Mass, and I expect your professors will direct you to them.

My own background is in literature and drama. At college I was a Speech and English major and my thinking is formed by the great English writers and dramatists. Before that I was an art student for a couple of years. Therefore, while I am not a liturgist or theologian, I do bring some knowledge of art, architecture, literature, myth, language, and dramatic theory to the table. Everybody comes to the church through a different gate, and that's the one I've come through.

I've also had the advantage of studying and working in England and traveling extensively in Europe. During those years I lived and prayed in some of the great buildings and locations. So I guess I soaked up a good bit of the great tradition, and that, along with being a Benedictine oblate, has informed my views.

So I decided to write you this series of letters on liturgy and other "churchy stuff." I don't pretend that my opinions are the final word. I expect they will annoy some people. Others may consider them simply eccentric, while others who are more expert than I will see my mistakes and omissions. They may do so, and I'm happy to accept their creative and positive critique. I'm not out to pick a fight. In the liturgy wars I am a pacifist, and I'm happy for people to disagree with me. These letters are just a way to share my opinions and experience—hoping that you might benefit from them as you continue to prepare for ordination.

You know me well enough to know that I am not a progressive. By this I mean I do not believe it is the Church's task to adopt the fashions and ideologies of each passing age. Instead, I believe the historic Catholic Faith offers the antidote to the candied poison of each passing age. While I'm not a progressive I am also not a fanatical traditionalist—thinking that the Second Vatican Council was the work of the Freemasons and Protestants in league with the Devil himself.

While I don't think the Church should adapt to every passing fad, I also think the gospel of Jesus Christ is ever ancient and ever new, so it does need to be accessible to modern Catholics, who for the last fifty years have been deprived of the liturgy in all its fullness. Just how that problem is to be solved is one of the great challenges. How do we stay rooted in the ancient and venerable traditions while still reaching out to people caught up in a fast-paced, hi-tech, ever-changing society?

With that in mind, I have to admit that I am not a gung-ho devotee of the Extraordinary Form of the Mass. I'm glad a wider permission has been granted for its celebration, and I have appreciated the Latin Masses I have attended, but I believe Pope Benedict's idea that the two forms of the Mass should inform each other is very wise. I worry that those who are exclusively attached to the Extraordinary Form of the Mass may be overly venerating a form of the Mass which has ossified, and that the traditions, as beautiful, reverent, and significant as they are, sometimes become an end in themselves rather than a means to an end.

I'm convinced that the Ordinary Form of the Mass, when celebrated reverently, in a way that is informed and influenced by the Extraordinary Form, can combine the best of our traditions, while still being accessible to most Catholics. This type of celebration also avoids the many abuses that too often accompany the Ordinary Form of the Mass.

Which brings me to the other side of the coin. If I'm

not a total fan of the Extraordinary Form of the Roman Rite, I'm definitely not a fan of the way the Ordinary Form is usually celebrated. Too many of our traditions of sacred art and architecture have been thrown on the scrapheap in the name of "Spirit of Vatican II." Sacred music has descended from the sublime heights to the drivel of pop music and folk songs. Reverence at Mass seems to be at an all-time low, and it is matched only by the banality of the preaching and the reduction of our glorious traditions to a bland mixture of sentimentality, trendy spirituality, and self-help. Sometimes I despair when I view the pews and see the faithful turning up to Mass chewing gum and wearing short shorts and tank tops… and that's just the guys!

I'm with the traditionalists when they lament the many abuses of the Ordinary Form. While it is true that the changes have helped the majority of Catholics understand Mass better, it is also true that, because of the dumbed-down form of celebration and catechesis, they understand the words but miss the meaning. Michael, I'm not writing these letters to get into a barroom brawl about rubrics with anyone. I'm sure there are good answers to the questions I have about liturgical abuses on both sides, but I'm more interested in the basics of our worship.

I've said my background is in art, drama, and literature, and one of the reasons I was drawn away from Protestantism and toward the Catholic faith was because of the beauty in Catholic liturgy and tradition. At first this was simply an aesthetic attraction. I liked the beautiful liturgy, music, vestments, art, and architecture. Then I came to realize that my attraction was to more than just "pretty things."

Our Christian faith is rooted in the incarnation of God's Son—the second person of the Holy Trinity, who took human flesh. Therefore, matter matters. The physical realm is not evil or of no consequence. "The heavens declare the glory of God, and the firmament shows his handiwork" (Ps 19). The whole created order shows God's creativity and we ourselves are "God's work of art" (Eph 2:10). From the beginning Catholics recognized this and insisted that art, architecture, music, poetry, and literature were not only permissible, but important. The creations of man's hands therefore reflected the creativity of God. Because Jesus Christ was the "icon of the unseen God" (Col 1:15), icons could help us move beyond words to wordless wonder.

It is no coincidence that Protestantism was invented at the same time as the printing press. Protestantism was the religion of the book, and thereafter Christianity became much more bookish, intellectual, and talkative. Catholicism was not spared this sad verbosity, and for the last five hundred years Catholicism has followed the Protestant lead and become more and more wordy and abstractly theological, more wedded to words, words, words.

As we have become more wordy we have forgotten the importance of the image, the icon, the symbol, and the sign. Everything has to be spelled out, defined, and defended. Ironically, at the same time our society has become less and less literate. We can read but we don't. Instead we are enchanted by the screen. Almost without noticing, we have become a visual people, not a literate people.

I believe this is actually a gain for the Catholics and Eastern Orthodox, because we, of all Christian groups, have a tradition of making the faith visual. Consider our great cathedrals, our sublime painters, our composers, iconographers, stained-glass artists, sculptors, artists, and architects. In every age Catholics have made beautiful temples for the Lord and celebrated Mass with visual and sensual beauty.

This is the advantage of our age and a great opportunity. Now is the time to build beautiful churches, commission artists who understand, build great choirs, and inspire and evangelize with very visual and beautiful Catholic worship.

Don't get me wrong: I'm not advocating beautiful Catholic worship simply as a gorgeous museum piece or an ecclesiastical fashion show. The beauty of Catholic worship has a point. It is iconic; and like every icon, the image communicates multiple levels of meaning without words. When I say traditional Catholic worship is iconic, what I mean is that every person, every action, every vestment, every point of art and architecture, music and liturgical text functions like an icon—a door into the invisible realm of God's presence.

So what is the point of the liturgy? The bottom line is that Jesus said at the Last Supper, "Do this in remembrance of me." So the Mass is a way of remembering Jesus. However, it is not simply a memory prompt or an indulgence in nostalgia about Jesus. We might "feel closer to Jesus" at Mass, but that's not really the main point.

The "remembrance" part of it is linked with the word *anamnesis*, which I'm sure you've already encountered at seminary. *Anamnesis* is a unique kind of remembering by which, through a ceremonial action, an event from the past is not simply re-lived but brought into the present moment so that we participate in it. It's kind of like time travel. By remembering Jesus's sacrifice on the cross we are zoomed back in time to that afternoon outside Jerusalem, and likewise that moment zooms forward in time to be alive and real on every altar where the Mass is celebrated. Someone has said that "the Mass expresses an eternal action in one place and time."

Maybe it is a bit like going to see a play by Shakespeare. Let's say you go to see a production of *Hamlet*. You don't go to simply study the language or watch the characters interact. The whole point of the play is that you are taken out of yourself and out of your time for a few hours and you are transported back to the castle of Elsinore in Denmark. As *Hamlet* is performed, those events (even though they are fictional) come alive and we participate in them. There, as you watch, you identify with the main character. You go on his journey with him and if the chemistry of drama works, you not only watch his actions but also feel his feelings. When Hamlet dies, a little bit of you also dies. When the drama works we experience "catharsis"—a profound inner encounter with the emotions and themes of the drama.

This is not a perfect example, because the Mass is not just a stage play by Shakespeare. Something greater is going on—but it is an analogy that helps explain what we mean by "anamnesis."

If I am right about this, then everything we do at Mass is subordinate to this one aim: to participate fully in the remembrance of what Jesus Christ has accomplished for us on the cross. More than that, the liturgy is also a participation in the eternal moment of worship in heaven. This "remembrance" is also a "looking forward to."

I've said that to "participate fully" is for us to engage body, mind, and spirit in this living act of remembrance. To do this is more complicated, and more beautiful, than it would first appear. I think many of the abuses in the Ordinary Form are a sincere attempt to get everyone involved and for everyone to "experience something" when they come to Mass. This often not only fails, but is manipulative; people sense that and the whole enterprise becomes counter-productive. Therefore, as a religious experience the result is either an artificial, shallow, and sentimental response or a simple rejection.

You have probably experienced the same thing I have. You go to worship, and they are playing songs that are supposed to make you feel some sort of religious feeling or other; instead of the magic working you feel manipulated, and reject the emotional music and the fake religious atmosphere. That sort of "worship" is a lame attempt

at entertainment—trying to force a manufactured religious response on people.

What should happen at Mass is much more subtle and
profound. When I say we should engage "body, mind, and
spirit" I mean that those three parts of us should be
authentically connected with the life-giving Spirit of God
through this act of remembrance, sacrifice, and thanksgiving. If God is a Holy Trinity, then the little holy trinity of
our Body, Mind, and Spirit should engage with the
greater Holy Trinity through the action of worship.

As members of Christ's body we share in his priestly
action, which is an eternal exchange of love between
Father, Son, and Holy Spirit. Love is the energy that binds
together the three persons of the Holy Trinity, and
through the liturgy we enter into that dynamic of eternal
energy.

I've said we can't just make this happen. The Father
does this work through Jesus Christ in the power of the
Holy Spirit. All we can do as we lead the worship is to
create the right atmosphere for this interaction to take
place. Church is therefore like a greenhouse. In a greenhouse the exact environment is created for seedlings to
flourish. In the liturgy celebrated within the whole communion of the Church, we are drawn into an environment
in which our people can engage with the saving action of
Christ fully for their own soul's salvation and the salvation
of the whole world. This is what the Mass is and does. This
is what Mass is for: the objective worship of God which
seals the salvation and sanctification of God's people.

2

Sacrifice
or Sacred Feast?

D<small>EAR</small> M<small>ICHAEL</small>,

You've been to all the parishes in our town, so you'll know how different they all are. At St Patrick's, Fr Carson celebrates the traditional Latin Mass whenever possible (with a paid choir singing Palestrina and Vivaldi), while down at Our Lady of Guadalupe Fr Juan welcomes a standing-room-only congregation of Hispanics who praise the Lord with guitars, accordions, clapping and loud praise, and worship songs in Spanish. Meanwhile, Fr Johnson at Our Lady of Fatima celebrates a solemn Novus Ordo Mass with English chant, traditional hymns, and solid preaching, while Fr Gordon SJ celebrates an informal Mass with a gospel choir and a hefty dose of political activism. Then there are the Byzantine Catholics, the Koreans, the Maronites, and the Anglican Ordinariate congregation.

A typical American parish is probably like Holy Name, where the building may well be a large, fan-shaped auditorium with padded pews, soft lighting, and a soft rock band up front to lead the music, but in most places you'll find a wide variety of worship styles—each one reflecting the personality and preferences of the people and the priest. The reality is that Catholics in America shop for their church just like they shop for everything else.

Is all this variety a healthy manifestation of a diverse and multi-ethnic Church or is it chaos leading to liturgical catastrophe? Is this range of choices simply the Catholic Church being successfully integrated with culture, or has the culture taken over and obliterated anything recognizably Catholic? Is all the variety a good thing or just a smoke screen for "anything goes" and "I'll do it my way"?

When you consider the global Catholic Church, the variety is even greater. Africans dancing together at the liturgy with drums and tribal music is a far cry from a solemn pontifical Mass in Latin in a baroque church in Rome. A papal Mass at World Youth Day is miles away from the contemplative otherworldliness of Mass in a traditionalist monastery. We recognize that it is all Catholic liturgy, so how do we begin to sift out what is good, what is better, and what is best—or does it really matter anyway?

I think it does matter. Some celebrations of the liturgy are better than others, and I believe there are some criteria that can help us discern what is more fully Catholic and what is not.

We should start with basic questions. What is the liturgy actually for? What is the Eucharist, what does it signify, and what does it effect?

The Mass is the remembrance of Christ's work on the cross, but it is actually more than that. The Catechism expresses a variety of understandings, all of which combine to give a basic explanation of what is going on at

26

Mass. As the Catechism teaches, the Eucharist is "the source and summit of the Christian life" (CCC, para. 1324). It is the breaking of the bread whereby the Lord is recognized and known. It is a sacrifice of praise and thanksgiving. It is a solemn banquet—a fellowship meal. It is a remembrance of the Last Supper, and both a foretaste and a participation in the worship of heaven. It is a celebration of church unity, but all of these aspects are gathered up in the primary meaning—a commemoration of Christ's work on the cross.

The re-presentation of Christ's once-and-for-all sacrifice—eternally offered at the right hand of the Father—must be the central focus of and reason for the Mass. There are several reasons why, but the first is that the principle of sacrifice is at the heart of humanity's shared experience of religion. We all know that one must make a sacrifice to achieve anything. You must die to self in order to live. We all know at the deepest level of our shared humanity that sacrifice is a turning point in our existence. Parents make sacrifices for the good of their children—giving their lives so that the children can live. Soldiers, firefighters, and police risk their lives and make sacrifices to protect and defend their people. The principle of sacrifice is written into all the great sagas, stories, legends, and myths of the world. The hero always sacrifices himself to complete his quest. Sacrifice is woven into the fabric of our history. The Sacrifice of the Mass echoes therefore in the deepest chambers of our hearts.

Furthermore, all other meanings of the Mass either

point toward the reality of sacrifice or derive from it. The sacrifice of Christ is the core truth and source of the other meanings. It is the sun around which they circle and from which they take their light. If this is so, then the priority of the sacrificial understanding of the Mass will help us assess the worthiness of our worship.

In primitive societies sacrifices were made to appease the gods so they would give mortals prosperity, peace, and protection. The Jews had a very complex understanding of sacrifice, and their system sheds light on the importance of sacrifice and what it means even today.

In the Old Testament there were six types of sacrifice. An oblation was an offering of cakes. A holocaust was a whole burnt offering. A bull would be killed and the whole carcass burnt on the altar. In a peace offering only the blood and fat of the sacrificial animal would be burnt. The rest would be eaten by the priest. A thank offering was an offering of wine poured out on the altar. This was also called a "sacrifice of praise." In the sin offering or offering of atonement two goats would be offered. The sins would be projected onto the goats. One would be killed. The other would be driven into the wilderness. This was the scapegoat. The final type of sacrifice was the Passover Lamb.

In a marvelous way Christ's sacrifice and the celebration of the Mass gather up all these types of sacrifice. We offer "cakes" and wine. Christ's death is the total holocaust of himself, and he is the one (like the scapegoat) onto whom mankind's sin is projected. Finally, he is the

Passover Lamb—the Lamb of God. His Paschal sacrifice re-capitulates and completes all the other sacrificial systems, both pagan and Hebrew, and it is his flesh we eat and blood we drink to re-establish peace with God.

Through sacrifice the door is opened to the spiritual plane, and by participating in this ritual we break through the barrier of our mortal finiteness to share in the eternal dimension.

Therefore, a celebration of Mass which unlocks and focuses on the sacrificial death of Christ on the cross and that eternal offering in heaven will be the highest and most complete celebration of Mass. A celebration that focuses primarily on the fellowship of the church, praise and thanksgiving, a political preaching point, or merely a memory of the Last Supper may not be completely wrong, but it will not have the correct priority.

However, since the second Vatican Council, much of the emphasis in both liturgy and catechesis has been toward the fellowship and social mission of the church more than the sacrifice of the Mass and the salvation of souls. There are many reasons for this, but one of them was that theologians and liturgists considered the concept of sacrifice to be primitive, barbaric, and inaccessible for modern people. As the Mass was translated into the language of the people, sincere liturgists and pastors were delighted that at last they could help the Faith become real and relevant. All the old ways with Latin, the priest facing away from the people, and the old devotions and prayers seemed out-of-date and out-of-touch.

The Mass came to be understood not so much as a sacrifice but more as a fellowship meal. This was not completely wrong. The roots of the Mass are in the ritual shared meals of the Hebrews. Theologians picked up on this and saw a greater modern accessibility in this aspect of the Mass. So the commemoration of the Last Supper became the prominent idea.

The worship was turned toward the people, toward fellowship, so that the people could be empowered to live in community and transform the world as Christ's salt of the earth. At the same time the ecumenical movement was a bright hope, and shifting the Mass away from sacrifice to fellowship meal was seen as a way to answer Protestant objections. This fundamental shift was therefore well-intentioned, but the radical new emphasis became the byword for a revolution in the church.

This is evident from changes in every aspect of church life: The word *table* replaced *altar*. The priest turned to face the people instead of offering the sacrifice with them and for them facing the Lord. Equality was in and hierarchy was out. Architects built flat, round churches that emphasized everyone gathering around the table of the Lord together. Gregorian chant, sacred polyphony, and pipe-organ music were considered out-of-date and inaccessible. Popular and folk music and pop-rock were thought to be more easily understood. Easy-to-sing hymns turned the people away from what seemed distant worship of God and devotion to the Blessed Sacrament and instead emphasized the worshiper's feelings, or stressed God's people gathering together and doing their good work in the world. The preaching began to focus more on social activism, spirituality, or personal therapy rather than sin, salvation, repentance, and redemption.

What they forgot in emphasizing the "fellowship meal" is that another sacred meal was also being commemorated and participated in. That is the marriage supper of the Lamb. In the Book of Revelation we get a glimpse of the worship in heaven, which is portrayed as a great marriage supper, and it looks very Catholic. There are angels and saints gathered around the altar. There is chanting, incense, and the triumphant worship of God. In emphasizing the fellowship meal and making Mass informal they forgot this other sacred meal, in which the worship is anything but a happy potluck supper.

The effect of this shift in emphasis has been devastating for the Catholic Church, because along with the revolution in the liturgy went a revolution in theology and practice. As the focus went from sacrifice to fellowship meal, the attention of the faithful went from a concern about their soul's salvation to the community's good works in the world. One's salvation seemed dependent not so much on repentance and participation in Christ's saving work on the cross as on one's involvement with the corporal works of mercy—feeding the hungry and working for peace and justice in the world. The shift therefore went from what God does in the liturgy to what we are doing in the world.

If this is so, then we have a basic foundation for assessing the different forms of liturgy. We should not judge according to the music we happen to like or dislike, nor should we judge solely on external things like vestments, candles, architecture, or art. We are not judging the worthiness of the worship according to our particular tastes, culture, or ethnicity. We judge according to the liturgy's focus on the passion and resurrection of the Lord—which lies at the heart of the Eucharistic sacrifice. The externals either help achieve that focus or hinder it.

While a beautiful, traditional celebration of the Extraordinary Form sets a kind of gold standard, it can't be imposed on everyone, nor should we assume an attitude of liturgical snobbery or superiority.

While the traditional celebration of the Mass is to be preferred, I have been to Masses in a village in El Salvador where the music was played by villagers on guitars and accordions. The people were clapping and singing their hearts out, dogs were wandering about in the church, while little children crowded the pews and babies were being breastfed. The music was loud and badly done and the building was a simple shed, but despite all this, the people were reverent and the priest celebrated the Mass with a quiet, dignified simplicity. The whole experience brought to life the poverty of Christ and the beauty and humility of his love for us—made real for us at his death and present in the Eucharist.

What about the priest who is suffering in constant pain in a wheelchair with his strength failing, the Mass celebrated by the chaplain on the hood of a jeep the day before battle, or the priest huddling with a few faithful, a scrap of bread, and smuggled wine in the horror of Auschwitz? These examples and many more reveal the beauty and humility of the Paschal passion of the Lord in other ways.

I'm pointing this out because surely the form of the Mass is important, but also we must realize that it is not the most important thing. Many different forms of celebrating the Mass can be reverent and bring us closer to the encounter with Christ, while many are deficient in this respect. We know that many different forms are permitted—not only the Extraordinary and Ordinary Forms, but also the rituals of the different ancient churches in communion with Rome. We also know that a vast array of cultural situations exist which impose huge variety on the way Mass is celebrated.

I don't want to fall into the trap of judging each of these liturgies according to my own feelings at Mass. However, those feelings should also not be ignored. I think we can say this—as long as its form is valid, the Mass objectively accomplishes what it signifies. No matter what the form or the variety of music, the liturgy brings us face-to-face with Jesus Christ both crucified and glorified. However, some styles of celebration help us experience this exchange better than others.

That being said, what are some things we can do to bring that celebration to the point where the focus is on the saving work of Christ, and what can be done to assist the people to that encounter with him which is the

33

"source and summit of our faith"? My other letters to you will be about these practicalities. Although I'm rather traditional in my own tastes, I believe that with pastoral care, an open mind, and some professional discernment, we can meet the vast variety of liturgical styles in our Church and bring them together so that, while we will not have uniformity, we will have a much better focus of unity.

But before I get to the practicalities I want to observe that a traditional celebration of the Mass—either the Extraordinary Form or the Ordinary Form informed and influenced by the Extraordinary Form—not only retains the eternal sacrifice of Christ as the main focus, but also helps to express and bring about Church unity in ways the other forms cannot.

Let me explain: the Extraordinary Form of the Mass is the Mass of the Ages and it therefore transcends particular time-periods and cultures. A traditional church building, Gregorian chant, traditionally trained altar servers, and a traditional style of celebrating the Mass rise above all our individual tastes, cultural influences, fashionable ideas, and political ideologies. The very antiquity of such a liturgy gives it a transcendence that cannot be denied.

Therefore, the observations that follow will show how a traditional celebration of liturgy can not only connect us with the timeless Mass of the Ages, but also transcend all the different cultures and ways of offering Mass that abound in the Church today.

3

Priest:
Wimp or Warrior?

EAR MICHAEL,
Have you noticed how blockbuster movies and
TV series so frequently feature a warrior as the
main character? Our society is supposed to be all sweet,
calm, and peaceful, but the movies thump it home that
heroes are warriors. It doesn't matter if it is a superhero
movie, a TV series about the Vikings, *Mission Impossible*, or
Star Wars—both explicitly and subtly, there is always a
battle and the hero is always a triumphant soldier.

After I left the Anglican ministry I trained as a script
writer, and one of the sources I studied was Joseph
Campbell's book *The Hero with a Thousand Faces*. Campbell,
brought up as a Catholic, studied the sagas and stories of
many different cultures. He discovered one story to rule
them all. In many different forms, it was the story of the
hero's quest. The hero was usually a warrior who set out
from his ordinary world to battle evil. What really interested me was that the hero would always come face-to-
face with the need to make a sacrifice.

In pagan stories the hero would make a sacrifice to the
gods, but in other stories he would have to make a personal sacrifice, giving up all for the sake of the quest, or

he may even have died in the battle, only to rise again in some magical way.

You might wonder what I'm getting at. It's this: I think the priest is also a classic hero and a warrior. But to make my point, I'd like to say a bit more about the concept of sacrifice.

The last time I wrote, I said one of the forms of Jewish sacrifice was the sin offering or the sacrifice of atonement. Twin goats were offered. One was killed as an atonement for sin. The priest then laid his hands on the head of the other goat projecting the actual sins of the people onto the goat. The goat was then driven into the wilderness to "take away the sins of the world."

What was going on in this primitive ritualistic action? To understand that we have to go further back into the origins of evil. The French thinker René Girard makes the point that human evil begins with a form of envy you might call "imitating desire." We not only desire what somebody else has—we want their power. We want to be like them. This essential flaw in our nature is shown right there in the old tale of the Garden of Eden. Eve wants more than the knowledge of good and evil. Satan tempts her by saying, "You will be like God!" In other words, she not only wants the knowledge that God has; she wants to be God.

This was Satan's own downfall, and it is the root of all evil. We want to be God. We want to be the author of our own destiny. We want to be in control. The problem grows, however, because we are not God. We therefore experience an inner restlessness and emptiness which causes us to look elsewhere with a constantly aching and searching desire, and when that desire is not satisfied we look around for someone to blame for our unhappiness. Again, we see this in the Garden of Eden. When God asked Adam why he had eaten the fruit, he blamed Eve, and when God asked Eve about it she blamed Satan. In fact, it's even worse than that—Adam actually blamed God for the problem. He said, "The woman YOU gave me gave me the fruit to eat."

This is a devastating insight. When we realize we cannot be that person we want to be like, we turn the tables and blame him for our unhappiness. As we do this we try to justify ourselves. We believe we are good, and since we are good, our problems can never be our fault; and if the problems are not our fault, someone else must be to blame. The one we blame is the one who has what we want, and when we can't have what he has we blame him for the problem and kill him.

This step is clear from the next story in Genesis, in which Cain kills his brother Abel. God asked for a particular form of sacrifice, but Cain decided to do things his own way. In disobeying God Cain puts himself above his maker. So God rejected Cain's disobedient offering and accepted Abel's. Then Cain—who was in the wrong—projects his sin onto his brother and blames Abel. He sees Abel as the problem and kills him. The conclusion is frightening: take God's place through disobedience and bloodshed is the result.

We blame others on an individual level, but we also blame others on the corporate level. A horrible dynamic emerges in which the group—suffering from some misfortune—blames someone else. That someone is invariably the outsider, the cripple, the foreigner, or the misfit. That person takes all the blame and they are first persecuted, then excluded. Then, when that doesn't work and they are still seen as the source of the problem, they are eventually killed. Now we can see what the two goats stood for in the Old Testament. They represent the two ways we constantly deal with our own sin. We project it on to someone else, and expel that person from our presence. We blame that person and, in effect, we "kill" him.

After the violence takes place, the group or the individual feels a sense of elation. They think the problem has been solved at last and there can be peace. The sting in the tail is that before long another problem arises. Another crisis crops up. What must they do? They find another victim and a pattern of persecution, exclusion, and finally murder takes place.

After a while this pattern of tribal behavior becomes ritualized, and the community finds release through ritual sacrifice. The ritual sacrifice develops into a religion and a symbolic animal is substituted for the human victim.

What can anyone do about this violence? Nothing. The person or group who blames others is invulnerable to criticism. They truly believe they are right. By the very nature of this insidious pride, the person or group blaming the scapegoat is self-righteous. Their pride prevents them from seeing that they have a problem. They cannot see that they are persecuting an innocent victim. They really believe that they are good, and the person they are blaming is the problem. Furthermore, if you criticize a self-righteous person or a group like that you will end up being one of the problems that needs to be eliminated!

Think of the violence shown to the victims of the Nazis, the victims of racism in the American South, the Christians who are martyred, or any other group of sacrificial victims. The crowd really believed the victims were the problem, and so to get rid of the problem they persecuted, excluded, and finally killed them.

This is the pattern of human evil in the world from the very beginning. The whole of sacred scripture is the story of mankind perpetrating this same pattern time and time again.

Only one thing can be done with this pattern of violence, and Jesus Christ reveals it. He steps up to the plate and says to Satan (who is the author of the violence): "I'll take it. You want to blame someone? Blame me. You want to reject someone as the scapegoat? I'll take it. You want to kill someone to solve the problem? Do you need a sacrificial lamb? Behold the Lamb of God." The high priest Caiaphas unknowingly admitted this when he said, "It is better that one man should die than many." By accepting the blame and going on his own to his death on the cross, and then rising again, Jesus takes the violence and defeats it from the inside out. Because he is God he has the authority to do that. Because he is man he takes on the whole of humanity. That's why he is the Lamb of God and why, in the Book of Revelation, the Lamb on the throne is the "Lamb who was slain."

By his death and resurrection, Christ reverses the cycle of violence begun right at the beginning with Adam and Eve's rebellion and Cain's murder of his brother Abel. As he does this Christ becomes both priest and victim, and this action is re-presented in the action of the Mass.

In the early Church and right up through the Middle Ages Christ was first and foremost seen, therefore, as the great warrior. He was the one who did battle with Satan on the cross. He was *Christus Victor*—the Victorious Christ. He was Christ the hero—the one who conquered death and hell by being the satisfaction and substitute for sin.

One of the things that annoys me most about the Church today is that Christ is portrayed not as the Victor, but as the weak martyr. It is true that Jesus is meek and humble of heart, but since the Romantic age in the nineteenth century, the images of Jesus have become increasingly feminized. His meekness has overwhelmed his majesty. Jesus has become a wimp, not a warrior. He's pictured with pretty robes and long blonde hair. Some of the worst images show him with long eyelashes and pink cheeks, cuddling a sweet little lambkin. Yuck!

Another kind of sentimental Jesus is the hippy pacifist. This image came into fashion in the 1960s. Jesus became a long-haired, effeminate preacher of peace. Jesus was drafted in to give a blessing to every kind of limp project, and as this happened a strange twist took place. Because

Jesus was a voluntary victim, it became fashionable to play the victim in order to gain sympathy. If you wanted to promote a cause, just make yourself out to be a victim and whine enough and you could bully others to get your way. Unfortunately, too many priests jumped on this bandwagon and made the Church into a wishy-washy organization of whining weaklings and manipulative crybaby bullies.

Which brings me to the question: is the priest a wimp or a warrior? I think he is a warrior—but not a warrior who is simply a gorilla macho man, or a dominating tyrant. Neither is he a warrior in an arrogant, aggressive, or violent manner. Instead, like Jesus Christ, whose image he bears, the priest is a knight who slays the dragon—a warrior against evil. He is one who, like Christ, steps up to do battle with the devil to the bitter end.

How does the priest do this? By being conformed to the image of Christ—and the terrible irony is that Christ is both priest and victim in the Eucharistic feast. Through ordination and his response in prayer, service, and self-sacrifice, the priest becomes an *alter Christus*. He identifies with Christ the Victor through the celebration of the liturgy, but he also identifies with Christ the Victim in the willing sacrifice of his life through his high vocation and calling.

You might wonder what the liturgy has to do with it. I'd say it has everything to do with it, for there the priest *in persona Christi capitis* takes up the timeless sacrifice and brings into the present moment the victory of Christ.

Through the action of the Mass the priest re-presents Christ's sacrifice through which he won the victory over death and hell. Through the sacrifice of the Mass Satan's defeat is made real once more.

Furthermore, it is through this constant re-presentation of the sacrifice of the cross that the priest and the people experience and participate in that victory. The whole people of God are called to live out this priesthood in the world. It is also through this profound participation that we receive the graces to continue living out that victory in the world. The power of Christ's flesh and blood shed on the cross and the power of his resurrection are made real and applied in the world at every altar and in every soul who is joined to the liturgy by faith and action.

This, then, is the heart of sacrifice—not making an offering in some vain effort to appease God or make him happy by giving him something. Christ's death does not pay a price to God in some primitive understanding of human sacrifice, nor is Jesus paying some sort of debt to a bloodthirsty God.

Instead Christ's death wins our salvation because Christ wrestles there with the very source and heart of human darkness. He confronts the cycle of blame and shame and takes on the violence of pride and defeats it with an embrace of love. When we say, "Jesus died to save us from our sins," this is what it means. He saves us from Sin— from that first source of sin in which we said, "We would be like God." From that attitude of pride all other evils grew like a poisonous and insidious vine, and it is that source of Sin that is defeated at the cross by Christ the Victor.

As we commemorate this sacrifice we commemorate the fact that the need for sacrificing the scapegoat has ended, and as a result we gain the power and determination to stand against all kinds of scapegoating and victimization.

This is why I contend that the priest must be a warrior, not a wimp. He is a man of sacrifice. He is one who hears Jesus Christ say, "Take up your cross and follow me," and "unless you take up your cross and follow me you cannot be my disciple." The way the priest does this is by offering the sacrifice of the Mass with due reverence and awe—realizing that through the blessed action the saving work of Christ is constantly made real in the world.

4

Celebration
of the Mystery

D EAR MICHAEL,
I had a wonderful time on my vacation retreat
last summer. I went to Quarr Abbey—a Benedictine monastery on the Isle of Wight in England. Quarr is a magical place where you can step out of the crazy pace of modern life and step into the peace and tranquility of the timeless Benedictine traditions. The monastery is a member of the Solesmes Congregation—a French branch of the Benedictines specializing in liturgy and Gregorian chant.

One of the monks was speaking with me about the liturgy and pointed out that the word *celebration* is rooted in the idea of visiting or re-visiting on a regular basis. We think of *celebration* as another word for a party, but in fact when we say we are celebrating a birthday, for example, we are revisiting or remembering that event, and the word therefore has a solemn and ceremonial connotation beyond simply balloons and booze, a cake, some speeches and dancing.

As I mentioned before, celebration of the Mass is therefore a revisiting of the saving work of Christ on the cross and at God's right hand in heaven. It is going back again and again and re-presenting and bringing into the present moment that once-for-all sacrifice. With this in mind, there ought to be some principles of celebrating the Mass that standardize this celebration.

The rubrics in the missals before the Second Vatican Council were very precise. They mandated exactly how the Mass was to be celebrated. Every gesture and word was specified and priests were not permitted to deviate in any way from what was prescribed.

I remember one priest joking that he had to pay close attention because every time he said Mass there was the chance that he might commit forty-three mortal sins if he made mistakes in the details of his celebration.

In many places the Ordinary Form of the Mass has now gone to the other extreme. There are not only far fewer rubrics, but the atmosphere of informal fellowship means priests feel free to take liberties not only with the actions and gestures of the Mass, but also with the very words of the Mass. Some Masses are so informal they almost feel like a TV talk show, with the priest as the stand-up comedian host. Meanwhile, some Extraordinary Form Masses seem so stiff and aloof that they feel cold, sterile, and legalistic. This objective celebration of the liturgy seems even more distant because so many Catholics have gotten used to the informal, entertaining style of celebration.

Is there any way to find balance in what seems to be a liturgical free-for-all? Do traditionalists who are devoted to the Extraordinary Form of the Mass really believe the way forward is for all Catholics everywhere to abandon the Ordinary Form and adopt the strict uniformity of the old Latin Mass? If they believe this, I think they are being unrealistic. On the other hand, is it really a good thing that the liturgy has become so relaxed and informal that every priest can pretty much ignore the rubrics, do as he pleases, and make it up as he goes along according to whatever he thinks is right for him and his people?

I think there is a middle way, and this is where Pope Benedict XVI's *motu proprio Summorum Pontificum*, which allows a wider celebration of the Extraordinary Form, becomes important. The reason for his decision was not a belief that the Extraordinary Form would one day take over, but that the Extraordinary Form and the Ordinary Form would be "mutually enriching." Pope Benedict, like Pope St John Paul the Great before him, understood that the reforms of the Second Vatican Council needed to be understood within a "hermeneutic of continuity" rather than a "hermeneutic of rupture." In other words, the reform needed to amplify and expand what we received from the two-thousand-year tradition of the church. There should be evolution, not revolution.

How could this work in the celebration of the liturgy? I think certain principles can be established, and I'll go on to lay these out in a moment, but the best foundation for this continuity would be for all of those training for the priesthood not only to learn Latin, but to learn how to celebrate the Extraordinary Form of the Mass. This should not be an extra, but a foundation for a priest's training.

If you were engaged in any other profession you would take time to learn the elementary principles and history of your profession. If you were going to be a doctor, part of your training would be to learn about the Hippocratic Oath and the history of the development of the scientific method and the history of medicine and surgery. If you were training to be a lawyer you would learn something of the history and development of law and the legal system, and if you were training to be an artist or teacher you would study the history of art and the development of education and educational theory. Likewise, all priests should not only study Latin, but learn how to celebrate the Extraordinary Form of the Mass.

If every priest in training around the world did this, there would be a shared foundation in liturgy that would provide a unified underlying structure for the celebration of Mass in different cultures and worship settings. A priest in the Brazilian barrios or in downtown Manhattan would be rooted in the same liturgical understanding and practice. A priest celebrating a youth Mass for a charismatic praise service would have a profound link with the priest celebrating Mass for a convent of enclosed nuns. Despite the external diversity there would be an underlying unity. There would be a foundational vitality rooted in the historic Mass that would ground the diversity within the Ordinary Form.

What would be some of the underlying principles? First, an understanding that the primary purpose of the liturgy is worship of God. This would seem obvious, but there is always a temptation to treat the liturgy as a means to an end rather than an end in itself. What I mean is that we take a utilitarian approach to the Mass. We come to see it as a way to build fellowship or catechize the faithful. We treat it as a way to encourage our people to be better Catholics, better parents, better spouses, or better citizens. We use it a gathering to promote peace and justice, a way to encourage people to help the poor, evangelize, or minister to the needy.

All these objectives may result from our worship, but they are not the reason for our worship. The liturgy is the best and fullest way to fulfill what Christ calls "the first and greatest commandment"—which is to love God. Everything else flows from that, and that is why we call the Mass both the "source and summit" of our faith.

Second, that worship is not an individualistic action. This is not my worship or your worship, but the worship of the Church. Therefore, anything which calls attention to itself in a showy way should be ruled out. The liturgy is not the time for the priest to be an entertainer, nor is it the time for lectors, ushers, musicians, or anyone else to perform. Because this is the action of the whole Church, nobody should stick out. In an orchestra, even if an instrument has a solo part it is still part of the whole orchestra and the whole piece of music.

The Mass is an objective action of the whole Body of Christ down through the ages in every place and at every time, both here on earth and in heaven. Our particular act of worship is a part of that whole continuous, eternal act of worship. Our individual action is therefore caught up in something far greater and more awesome.

Nevertheless, there are individual benefits and graces that come from this cosmic action of worship. When we worship we place ourselves in right relationship with God, and when that placement is correct, everything else soon falls into its rightful place as well. When worship is first in our lives, our priorities are established and our other attachments and inordinate desires will soon fall into line accordingly. So, for example, if we love money too much, in true worship we come to love God first and we therefore desire to tithe, and that helps us put money in the right place. If we are prone to lustful desires, by putting God first and yielding the fleshly desires to God He will, in time, correct our lesser desires and align them to his will.

The third principle flows from the first two. If liturgy is the action of the church in worship, and if it is a foretaste and a share in the worship of heaven, then an atmosphere of reverence is vital. If you want to get an idea of the atmosphere of heavenly worship, read the Book of Revelation, chapter four. You'll find it is full of multitudes falling down in awe before the very throne of God. The reverence is as thick and pure as the incense rising. A reverent atmosphere can be nurtured in many practical ways, and it is a principle of Catholic worship that should be observed no matter what the cultural expression or form of the Mass.

Silence is necessary for an atmosphere of reverence. All

the small actions of priest and people either encourage or discourage reverence. Do we make the sign of the cross as a hurried wave of the hand, or do we take time and make the sign with meaning and purpose? Do we genuflect with a little head bob or with a profound bow and a true bending of the knee? Do we cultivate sacred silence within the celebration of Mass by reciting the words slowly and allowing space for silence to be developed? Do we nurture a culture of Eucharistic adoration in the parish? All of these little things help to develop reverence.

One of the most instrumental factors in developing reverence at Mass is how we receive communion. While the faithful can certainly be reverent in receiving communion in the hand while standing, no one can disagree that receiving communion on the tongue while kneeling is more reverent. Why is this? Firstly, because kneeling in our Western culture is an intrinsic act of devotion, homage, and worship. This is true no matter what the context. Knights kneel to receive their knighthood from the Queen. Bride and groom kneel to receive a nuptial blessing. To receive communion on the tongue is a sign of belief in the real presence of Christ's Body and Blood in the Eucharistic host, because a sign that you are intent not to profane the Body of Christ by dropping it or soiling it in any way.

A fourth basic principle for bringing a sense of unity to the celebration of the Mass is an affirmation that the Mass is a solemn and public ceremony or ritual. If to "celebrate" means to "revisit," then the repetitious nature of ceremony and ritual is important. Our body language and movement in the liturgy speak ceremonially. The priest and servers move more slowly and deliberately. Their actions are simple, noble, formal, and dignified—neither pompous and overly robotic, nor casual, quick, and sloppy. The priest's words and gestures when celebrating the Mass are the same each time. Formal repetition lifts the Mass into the realm of ritual and allows it to become familiar to us even as it transcends mere familiarity.

There are several reasons why this is important: first, because the ritualistic words and actions remove the person's personality from the equation. When a soldier in uniform stands to attention and salutes he is not Harry Johnson—the red-haired kid down the street. He is a soldier in the King's regiment. His personality disappears into his ceremonial role and he becomes a player in a much more important theater of action.

Likewise, when the priest solemnly crosses himself and intones, "In the name of the Father, the Son, and the Holy Spirit," his personality is subsumed into the role of the priest, allowing the heavenly realities to break through and become apparent. But when Fr Bob says, "Welcome to St Hilda's. How are y'all doing? It's a beautiful day and our celebration today is full of joy, so let's all turn and say good morning to each other!," Fr Bob, for all his sincerity, becomes the center of attention and has become more like an event organizer than a priest.

However, the more important reason for the liturgy to be ceremonial in style is because it is through ceremony and ritual that we connect with what I call the "deep-down things." I want to write to you further about this, but for now let me say that the liturgy is ceremonial, ritualistic, repetitive, and ancient. Through the ritual we connect with the ancient truths in a symbolic and unspoken way, and it is through this language that we worship best. It is through this language of worship that we not only open up to the deep-down things but also open up to the great, high things.

There are other principles that can bring unity to our worship without absolute uniformity, but they have to do with music, art, and architecture, and I don't have time to write more about that now. I'll send you my thoughts on those matters later.

Therefore, Michael, if you're not already learning Latin and learning how to celebrate the Extraordinary Form of the Mass I suggest you do so. No matter what parish you go to and what style of Mass you are asked to celebrate, if you learn the Extraordinary Form it will not only inform and influence every Mass you celebrate; it will bind your own celebration of Mass more firmly to the Mass of the ages and link all that you do as a priest more deeply with the eternal worship of God now and in every time and place throughout all ages.

5

On the
Mystery of Language

DEAR MICHAEL,
From my last letter you might imagine that I don't think the outward form of the Mass matters much. I do think it matters, but perhaps not in the way some people think. I think the form matters because the form is crucial for experiencing the mystery of the Mass. I wonder how many times you've heard me say, "a mystery is something that can be experienced, even if it cannot be explained." It's one of my favorite sayings, and I repeat it because I think it's worth repeating.

Language is the stuff of liturgy, but before we talk about anything else, I think it's worth pondering language itself rather than taking it for granted. If we understand what language does in the liturgy we'll begin to get why the form and style do matter.

The first and most basic use of language is for simple communication. When we say, "I need a sandwich," the meaning is simple and clear. But language does much more than communicate a straightforward, clear, and direct meaning.

As I've said, the liturgy for Catholics is like a living icon. In the liturgy we use symbolic language. So, for example, we refer to Jesus as "the Lamb of God." We use allusion and subtext so that a simple phrase carries many levels of meaning, and connects us with much more than the surface level of the words. Similarly, when we refer to "Abraham, our Father in faith," in one phrase we summon up the whole saga of Abraham, his relationship with God, and the whole subsequent history of the Hebrew people. The subtext of a phrase like "who takes away the sins of the world" is the whole theology of the atonement. Thus the language of the liturgy is rich, poetic, and deeply meaningful. But there is even more to it.

The style of the language we use evokes a mood. The latest English translation of the Mass uses an exalted style of language, with some archaic words like "beseech" and syntax that sounds formal and dignified. This was no accident. The translators were attempting to capture the sense of liturgical language by using an exalted style of English. This is not hip-hop street lingo, but neither is it quite so exalted and archaic as the language, say, of the Anglican Book of Common Prayer, which was written in the seventeenth century.

Why have a more exalted style of language for the liturgy? Not only to dignify our worship, but as part of an overall effort to lift ourselves from this world to the threshold of the next. Catholic worship is meant to bring us to the gate of heaven, and the exalted and sacred language is one of the things that helps this transition to take place. Those who argue for the use of Latin make the same point: the ancient nobility of the language lifts us from the mundane to the mysterious, from the everyday to the eternal.

The exalted style of language calls for a style of delivery that is exalted but not pompous. There are few things worse than a priest who has developed a stained-glass voice. When saying Mass we should speak slowly and clearly, with simple dignity and solemnity—neither exaggerating in a lofty way nor mumbling or dashing through the Mass without giving due weight and reverence to the words we are speaking.

Michael, I hope in seminary they give you at least a smattering of speech training so you are able to project your voice, use clear diction, and speak the words of worship with simple dignity and manly grace.

But what interests me most about language is something more than all this. Have you ever seen one of those graphs where they chart the spectrum of light waves known to man and the width of sound waves, and then along those two graphs they show the amount of light and sound humans can perceive? It's tiny compared to the whole range of light and sound.

In other words, there is much more in the world of light and sound than we can perceive. Likewise, there is much more to the human person than we are aware of and can talk about. There are realms of the human person that are beyond language. Think of it like this: you existed before you learned how to talk. For nine months you were in your mother's womb and for another two years you existed without language. We can call this state of being "sub-linguistic." It is a time in your life without language.

Nevertheless, this was a very important stage in your life. In fact, it is arguable that this is the most vital stage of life because it is the time when the foundations are laid for your personality and future experience. That sub-linguistic stage of existence was experienced and perceived without words, and if it was without words it was also without logical order and structure. That stage of existence is pure instinct and emotion. Furthermore, at that stage things happened in your life which remain down deep in the sub-linguistic part of your memory and personality.

The sub-linguistic is also the realm of our dreams; for the most part we experience dreams through emotion—visually and without language. The sub-linguistic is also the area of our existence that psychologists call the "collective unconscious." That part of our being is vast, deep, and uncharted. In that primeval place the language is one of signs, symbols, and archetypes.

In addition to this wordless, sub-linguistic aspect of your life, I believe there is also a "supra-linguistic" experience of which humans are capable. This is not a realm *below* the range of language, but above and beyond it. This supra-linguistic realm is experienced in various ways. People who speak in tongues at charismatic meetings shift over into a kind of gibberish talk which seems to be above rational language. Some say they are speaking in a heavenly language, and St Paul mentioned that he spoke in the "tongues of angels" (1 Cor 13:1). I believe the supra-linguistic realm is most often experienced in the silence of contemplative worship. It is there that we communicate with the Lord in the depth of the heart above the structure and limitations of ordinary language. It is in this silence that the mystics tell us they commune most vividly with the Lord, and it is in this sacred silence that we speak in the language without words—heart speaking to heart.

Why is this important? Because worship is both the pathway to heaven and a little glimpse of glory here and now. Worship is the way we step into the other side of reality. This is vital because we human beings need to get down to that sub-linguistic level—and up to that supra-linguistic level. We need to get down to the sub-linguistic level so that God can heal and touch that very deepest foundational level of our lives. We need to get up to that supra-linguistic level so that we can have the highest and holiest communion with God in the realm beyond language.

How do we do that? I believe worship is the mechanism by which we allow God's love to penetrate down to our deepest level and take us up to the highest level with him. Worship is how this transaction takes place, and it is the mystery of language, sign, and symbol which allows that communion and that communication to take place.

So how does it work?

It is not easy or automatic, because to maintain the boundaries of our sanity we keep the sub-linguistic level firmly locked away. Think of your life as a house with a haunted cellar. That's the sub-linguistic part of your being.

We keep the door to the cellar closed and locked. Similarly, the supra-linguistic level is usually inaccessible because our minds are more occupied with earthly matters.

First we should consider how we access the sub-linguistic level. One of the ways is through repetitious prayer, like the rosary. The repetition occupies, if you like, the linguistic channel of our brain, allowing the sub-linguistic level to be unlocked. By occupying the conscious level through repetitious prayer, the subconscious level is opened. Of course the holy rosary is not our only repetitious prayer. The liturgy itself is repetitious. We say the same words day in and day out, we go through the same words week by week, and the repetition pounds away occupying our conscious thoughts, while the door is opened for the Holy Spirit to bring healing to the sub-linguistic level.

The other kind of action that opens the sub-linguistic level is the ritualistic or ceremonial. Just as the repeated words in repetitious prayer occupy the conscious level, so ceremonial actions produce an opening to the deepest level of our soul. This is why, in the liturgy, doing things the same way each time, with the same ritualized gestures and actions, helps the transaction of worship to take place.

After many years of celebrating Mass and observing the results in my own life and the lives of others, I am convinced of the truth of these theories. The repeated words, actions, and gestures of liturgy echo in our minds and embed in our memories like a well-loved piece of music, and as they do, they seep deeply into the very core of our being.

But there is more. The language of the sub-linguistic level is that of signs, symbols, and archetypes. Certain types of people occupy the dream-level of our existence: a king and queen, a mother and father, a serpent or monster, a dark lord, a child, a warrior, a witch or a wise man, an angel or a demon.

These symbolic character types also recur in the biblical sagas, the Gospel stories, and the liturgy of the Church. When we encounter these types in films, drama, and literature they resonate with some of the deepest parts of our human existence. The same thing happens in the liturgy. In the liturgy and the sagas of sacred scripture certain symbols and types recur and echo in the caverns of our hearts and the depth of our imagination connects and interacts with them at the sub-linguistic level.

I want to write to you about this further in another letter, but let's leave it there for now. You might ask, what about the supra-linguistic level? If the repetition and ceremonial worship help us get down to the level below language, what helps us rise to the level above language? This is where my comments about Latin and charismatic worship echo back to me.

Anyone who has learned a foreign language knows that as you learn the new language you also learn to see the world in a completely fresh way. Everything becomes new as you master the new way of speaking. A foreign language transcends our everyday speech and experience.

As I said, this is what the charismatics witness to. When they speak in tongues they feel they are using language to transcend language. I believe the same thing happens when we use Greek or Latin in the liturgy. We're not all charismatics, but most of us are speaking in an unknown tongue! When we speak Greek in the *Kyrie Eleison* or Latin in the *Agnus Dei*, *Sanctus*, or *Gloria*—just a few moments in the liturgy—our language is transcending our ordinary language and showing us the world through a fresh filter. We connect with the emotional meaning of the words even if we do not connect with the literal meaning. So we are lifted into the supra-rational part of our mind, brought into that higher place where our hearts are joined in a greater language of worship.

This is one of the reasons why the Church instructs us to retain Latin in the liturgy. This is why I think Latin should be taught in Catholic schools and why I'm glad that those who are called to preserve the Latin Mass are able to do so with freedom and enthusiasm. I'm afraid I don't see the whole Mass being in Latin as the desired norm to be used by all everywhere. Why? Because the use of English for most of the Mass—especially for the readings—continues to make the Mass intelligible for most people. This is important not only so God's people can understand what is going on, but also for this subtle play between the linguistic level of our experience and the sub-linguistic and supra-linguistic.

What I'm getting at is this: to get to the sub-linguistic you have to go through language. The repetitious words that we understand are the gateway to that deeper realm which is below language. Likewise, it is the spoken words we understand which contrast with the Latin and Greek phrases that open our minds and hearts to the supra-linguistic level. The linguistic level is therefore the gateway to both the sub-linguistic and supra-linguistic.

This is shown even more by the other way we experience the supra-linguistic—and that is through sacred silence.

An old priest was once asked how long he prays. He said, "Two minutes, but it takes me twenty minutes to get there." What he meant was that he spent two minutes in rapt contemplation in the beautiful silence of God's presence. However, for the first twenty minutes he was probably praying the Divine Office and other vocal prayers. The twenty minutes in the realm of language took him to the realm beyond language.

This is why I believe the Novus Ordo Mass in English is important. We enter into the realm beyond words through words. It is through the language that we understand that we can move beyond that language.

Finally, there is one other very important key to unlocking the supra-linguistic level of our human experience: music. By its very nature music is both sub-linguistic and supra-linguistic. Someone has said that music is "emotion expressed as sound." Music opens the sub-linguistic realm which is the realm of wordless emotion because pure music is wordless emotion. Sacred music opens the supra-linguistic realm as the music combines with words to take us beyond words. I'll write more about that later, but for now, you might think all this is just a lot of psychological mumbo-jumbo or hogwash. You might ask what evidence I have for these theories. I'd reply that I have the evidence of being a priest for twenty-five years—fifteen as an Anglican and ten as a Catholic. During that time I have experienced deep healing at that foundational level of my life, and I've also experienced the knowledge of the presence of God in that higher frame of mind.

Furthermore, I've seen the same results in the lives of many ordinary Catholics. Are they aware of these categories of linguistic, sub-linguistic, and supra-linguistic? Of course not. They don't need to be. What I am explaining is going on all the time within them and through them in ways beyond their conscious knowing—and that's what you'd expect, because the sub-linguistic and supra-linguistic is just that—the realms beyond our conscious knowing.

Why do I believe this is happening? Because I see my people coming to the liturgy. They are participating at the deepest and highest levels of their beings simply by being there and sharing in what is going on. The foundational level of their lives is being touched, healed, and made whole through the action of the liturgy. I see them kneeling in silence and communing with the Lord, and I know they are also experiencing a hint of that higher level of communion with Him.

The beauty of this is that it is so ordinary! As a priest it is great if you are aware of these principles and aware of what is going on below the language and above the language, but even if you are not aware of what is happening, it is still happening, and it is all the more powerful for not being conscious. The fact that the foundation of our souls is being healed and the height of our humanity is being exalted while we are unaware of it is the beauty of the working of God's grace.

I believe God's grace works within us and for our healing most effectively when it is done in secret. Sometimes we are aware of his work, but God is always busy in our lives patching things up, smoothing things out, burrowing deep down to put things right, and lifting up our souls to make us all that we were created to be.

6

Words, the
Word and the World

DEAR MICHAEL,

I hope I didn't throw you in the deep end in my last letter with all that talk about "sub-linguistic" and "supra-linguistic." I know my theories are just that—theories that can't be proven. At least, they can't be proven with scientific experiments, but as I said, I think they can be shown from human experience.

One of the great things about being a pastor as opposed to being a theologian is that you see all the theories being lived out in the stresses and strains of ordinary lives. In other words, the practical reality of parish life also reveals which theological theories and psychological systems are only a clutch of clever ideas without any real substance.

Speaking of practical realities, the Liturgy of the Word is the part of the Mass where there is not much room for symbolism, or sub-linguistic or supra-linguistic connections. The gestures, the procession, and the ritual actions are visual, but the reading of the Word is just that: the Word. Because it is language it communicates verbally, not visually. There is a verse in the Bible that states it: "The Word of God is sharp and powerful as a two-edged sword" (Heb 4:12). This is the time when the truth should be understood and spoken clearly and unambiguously. If this is the underlying principle of the Liturgy of the Word, then I think everything else about the Liturgy of the Word follows clearly.

But before I get down to more practical matters, it is worth remembering that the Word of God is just that: the Word of God and not our words. We don't believe the Bible is inspired the way Muslims and Mormons believe the Koran and the Book of Mormon are inspired. They think their holy book was dictated to their prophet by an angel. Our belief in inspiration is more subtle and dynamic. It starts with the mystery that Jesus Christ is the Word of God incarnate.

Logos—the Word—is a Greek philosophical term for the creative power of God. You remember the Christmas Gospel reading from the beginning of John: "In the beginning was the Word, and the Word was with God, and the Word was God . . . and the Word became flesh and dwelt among us." Christ is the Word made flesh, and the sacred scriptures are the inspired written witness to that Word. He is the primary revelation. The Bible is the record of that revelation. The scriptures are sometimes referred to as the Bread of Life, and again, the link between Jesus the Bread of Life and the Bread of the altar is no coincidence, for they are all part of the same unity.

Dei Verbum—the Second Vatican Council document on the Word of God—says that "the scriptures are to be venerated with the same veneration as the Bread of the altar," and this is nothing new. St Ignatius of Antioch said the gospel was his refuge "like the flesh of Jesus." Origen wrote, "the bread Christ says is His Body is the Word that nourishes souls," and Tertullian affirmed, "The Word of Life is like the flesh of the Son of God."

Something powerful is going on here. Through the inspiration of the Holy Spirit, the Word who was made flesh was made word again—human words. The scriptures bear witness to Christ not only because they tell his story in many different ways, but because they are inspired by his Holy Spirit.

Within the living witness of the Church, the authors of the scriptures were inspired. The inspiration of the scriptures themselves ceased at the death of the apostles, but the guidance of the Holy Spirit in the Church is a continuous and ongoing process. The apostles and their close associates were inspired to write the Bible, but their successors were also led by the Holy Spirit to select the books that went into the Bible. Through the Holy Spirit the bishops, theologians, and scholars—and indeed the whole Church—are inspired to search the Scriptures, to interpret and preach the Scriptures. Through the Holy Spirit, preachers are inspired to study and preach; and all of us are inspired to open our ears to hear the Word of God and our eyes to read the Word of God.

This is why the Liturgy of the Word is important—because through the written Word of God we are connecting with the One who is the Word of God incarnate. To put it plainly, the scriptures bear credible witness to Him. Therefore, from a practical point of view, every effort must be made for the Scriptures to be read clearly and for the people to be able not only to hear but also to follow along as they read. One of the problems in the Church is that too often people are chosen to read the scriptures at Mass for the wrong reasons. You know the man or woman who gets a bit puffed up because they have an important role to play, or maybe a child who is chosen to read as some sort of reward for good behavior or achieving a certain level at school.

The primary reason to choose a reader is because they are a good reader. By a good reader we mean they should read clearly, loudly, and slowly. They should also avoid being overly dramatic and "meaningful." They should not read the scriptures as if they are doing a dramatic reading. That draws attention to them and not to the word of God. But neither should they read in a monotone, and although some people think the scriptures should be chanted, I think for most congregations that is alien and distracting, and most readers, priests, and deacons will find it daunting. In most cases simple, clear reading is what works best.

Why is that? Because the Word of God is the Bread of Life. It's not a fancy French pastry. We should remember that bread is a simple, wholesome food best baked plainly and served plainly, hot and fresh. This is where we stop to hear the word of God and think things through, and for us to do this the word needs to be spoken clearly and preachers need to preach clearly and simply.

I really get passionate about this point: that the Word of

God is not abstract theology, obtuse philosophy, or ethereal spirituality. Apart from the words of the prophets and the epistles of the New Testament, most of the portions of the Word of God are stories about God's relationship with His people. Stories are truth fleshed out. The abstract theological truths, doctrines, and moral teachings are illustrated concretely in stories.

The epistles and words of the prophets are not stories as such, but they are words that are written or spoken to real people in real-life situations. The prophets speak God's truth to God's people in particular historical moments. Likewise the epistles speak to particular people in real places with real struggles. This is vitally important to note, because we often reduce the scriptures to nothing more than proof-texts for doctrines or a rule book for the faithful.

If we remember that the scriptures are real-life stories or words written to address real-life situations, this part of the Mass will be more pastorally relevant and in contact with our people, and it will instruct us in the proper approach to the homily.

Which leads me to preaching. Why are so many Catholic homilists so bad at their job? I think it is because they feel obliged to turn the stories of the scriptures into doctrine to be believed and rules to be obeyed, or else they go to the other extreme and turn them into sentimental spiels about how to be nicer people or make the world a better place. In other words, they turn the word of God into nothing more than a dogmatic textbook, a moral rule book, or a feel-good self-help manual. It is much more than these. It is the witness to God's supernatural and ongoing relationship with his people—a witness that is dramatic, dynamic, and disturbing.

I think our preaching should bring this out. It should be the point where the readings connect with the lives of our people in a dramatic, dynamic, and disturbing way. It is dramatic because it should have an element of conflict. It should be dynamic because it is powerful, and it should be disturbing because it stirs up the complacent and disturbs the indifferent. What's that old saying? "The faith should be comforting to the distressed and distressing to the comfortable." Good preaching does just that.

Here are some simple pointers for good preaching: to make it dramatic, look for the conflict in the story and highlight it. There may be conflict between human characters, or between human and divine characters. It is in this tension that the interest lies and the truth is revealed. Furthermore, when we explore the richness of the paradox, poetry, allegory, and multiple levels of meaning, the liturgy of the Word becomes powerful.

For preaching to be powerful it needs to come from a heart on fire. The only way for the heart to be on fire is for it to be filled with the Pentecostal fire of the Holy Spirit. Therefore, pray throughout your preaching preparation, and pray for courage. The way for the homily to be disturbing is for it to be true. Do not aim to upset anyone. Simply pray to preach the truth courageously, and it will be disturbing enough. If the homily is disturbing in the right way, then it brings your hearers to a point of clarity and the point of choice. They see the right way, and they choose to follow that way or they do not.

If you want to be clear in your speaking and writing, the very best person to read is C. S. Lewis. Not only is he a wonderfully clear writer, but he writes boldly, with a sense of humor and a real sense of humility. If you want to catch the secret of his clear and disturbing style, check out a talk he gave to future preachers. Here are a few basic points I've learned from Lewis:

Remember you are speaking to ordinary folk. They're not stupid, but they are also not as educated in the faith as you are.

Avoid theological and ecclesiastical jargon and specialized language. Translate difficult terminology. Speak of "the historic faith" rather than "Chalcedonian Christology." Say "Christ is here under the form of bread and wine" instead of "reflect upon the holy mystery of transubstantiation." Avoid foreign terminology. It alienates people and makes you look like a snob. Speak of "the troubles of our day," not "the difficulties *de nos jours*."

Avoid intellectual references, attributions, and quotations. If you quote Dante or T. S. Eliot just do so without saying, "As the great poet T. S. Eliot has said..."—that sounds uppity. If you quote someone famous, your educated listeners will get it and think themselves smart for doing so. Those who don't will appreciate it for the quotation itself—not because you're a clever person who can quote learned writers.

Use short words and sentences. This aids clarity and gives your homily force.

Preach from the heart and from experience. Of course there will be theology and spirituality woven in, but the people need to see and hear how the faith is real in the lives of real people. Faith stories incarnate theology. Faith stories make real the truths you are preaching.

Finally, the Liturgy of the Word and the Liturgy of the Eucharist are not separate. The Old Testament points forward to Christ the Lord and the New Testament points back to him. Both bear witness to the Lamb of God. In the same way the Liturgy of the Word is the preparation for the Liturgy of the Eucharist. Just as the whole liturgy centers on the action of the altar, so every homily should lead up to a conclusion that points the people to the altar.

I remember a pulpit in a church in England where the woodworker carved some words in the desk where the preacher's notes would be placed. The words were from John 12:21, in which some people came to the disciples and said, "Sir, we would like to see Jesus." It was a reminder that the Liturgy of the Word and our preaching are for one thing and one thing only—to show Jesus. Someone else has said our preaching should be like those paintings of John the Baptist. He is always shown with one finger pointing to Jesus and saying, "He must increase and I must decrease."

It's a reminder that the Liturgy of the Word points to the Word made flesh, and therefore also to the altar where the Word is made flesh under the appearance of bread and wine. The Liturgy of the Word is the point where the people know and understand that this mystery of the Word becoming flesh is also a mystery alive in their own day-to-day lives.

7

Plays and Playtime

EAR MICHAEL,

Have you ever watched one of those British royal weddings? I watched one recently, and as I was watching the pageantry I asked myself why this spectacle is so fascinating for millions of people. It was more than the fact that they could ogle celebrities for an hour or so. There was something deeper going on, and it hit me that part of the fascination was the fact that this was a ceremonial, liturgical event.

For all the secularity of England—and our whole modern world—here was a church service to which millions of people were glued. What was the attraction? There was something dramatic about the event, and by "dramatic" I mean having to do with drama. It was like something out of Shakespeare or a fairy tale.

Think about it. There was the warrior prince in his military uniform. There was the bride—like Cinderella plucked from obscurity. The press has made Prince Andrew's daughters into the two ugly sisters (and when Harry and William were younger painted Prince Charles's wife Camilla as the wicked stepmother). The Archbishop played the wise spiritual mentor while the Queen and Prince Philip reign above it all as the majestic and noble monarchs. Maybe you think this sounds silly, but writers like Joseph Campbell, G. K. Chesterton, J. R. R. Tolkien, C. S. Lewis, and Bruno Bettelheim have taught us that fairy tales and myth are serious business.

Through fairy tales and myth we connect with the deeper parts of our humanity where archetypes and symbols are the common language. Through the royal wedding millions of people—without being aware of it—were connecting with that same deep level. They were connecting with their longing for a king and queen, the need to be adopted into a royal and noble family, the need for a noble warrior or a beautiful princess, the need to be loved and married in the sight of all and with the blessing of God.

My amazement that all of this was being played out on our screens at the beginning of the twenty-first century—proving that the power of myth, fairytales, and drama is just as mysteriously stirring and powerful as it has ever been. The popularity of superhero movies and television programs and of fantasy novels proves my point. These are our versions of the ancient myths being re-enacted and celebrated in our day.

That this was a church service brought home to me that there is something important here about the liturgy. I guess you know that in the ancient world drama developed as part of the rituals of worship. Greek religious ceremonies involved a liturgy with priests in special vestments, particular actions and gestures, and ritualistic words, chants, spells, and invocations.

The stories of the gods and goddesses began to be enacted on stage as part of the religious ceremonies. Liturgy and drama therefore share the same ancient roots.

What really interests me is a conversation C. S. Lewis had with his friend J. R. R. Tolkien. You probably know both men were not only great writers themselves, but were fascinated by the way ancient peoples connected with their stories. They did not just read them for entertainment. They recited them and listened to them in a ceremonial way. Furthermore, Lewis and Tolkien understood that through symbols and signs, ancient myths had a power to connect with the deepest parts of the human heart and imagination. The moment of enlightenment which led to C. S. Lewis's conversion was Tolkien's explanation of myth in the Gospels. He showed how the stories of the Gospel worked in the same way to touch the depths of the human heart. Lewis observed that the story of Jesus Christ worked like all the ancient myths, except that it really happened!

It was through religious ritual, drama, and ceremonial storytelling that the ancient peoples participated in the deep truths locked in the myths, and it is through the liturgy that we do a kind of ceremonial storytelling that connects us at the deepest level with the life-changing drama of Jesus Christ.

Within the action of the Mass, the Passion, Death, and Resurrection of Christ is not so much re-enacted (although this is obvious during Holy Week when the Passion narrative is read dramatically) as it is re-presented in signs, symbols, gestures, and actions. Furthermore, the congregation participates in the drama of the liturgy in a way that is similar to the participation of the audience at a film or the public performance of a play.

What exactly happens when you join the audience of a play or movie? The writers, directors, actors, and technicians all work together to bring you to the point where a kind of transaction takes place. You identify with the hero of the story, and a good storyteller works his magic so that you not only identify with the hero but sympathize with him. In other words, you bond with the hero through your emotions.

As the hero goes through his ups and downs you not only go through the pitfalls and victories with him—most importantly, you share his feelings. You gasp in surprise and terror when he sees the villain. You laugh with relief and joy when he rescues the fair maiden. You might even be brought to tears at a sad or especially beautiful part of the film or play. This empathy or "feeling-with" is part of the excitement of drama for both the audience and the players.

The same kind of participation takes place in the celebration of the liturgy. Of course it is not as highly dramatic as a play or movie. It's not supposed to be. The drama and the empathy take place at a much deeper level. Nevertheless, the kind of transaction is the same. When the liturgy is celebrated with care, beauty, and heartfelt devotion, emotional participation can be very profound. The documents of the Second Vatican Council call for the people of God to participate fully in what is going on at Mass. This kind of very deep participation is what the Council fathers meant by the phrase—not a superficial attempt to give everyone a job to do at Mass.

There is more to this, and it has to do with the Church as the Body of Christ. We are a communion or a family of believers. We are not alone. No man is an island. Instead we are one in the Lord. St Paul says this: "We who are many are one body for we all share in the one bread" (1 Cor 10:17). This is more than a symbol—for the Church, in a very real way, *is* the Body of Christ.

This is more than just a beautiful idea or a theological theory. It is understood when we turn again to the liturgy as drama. Have you ever noticed, for example, that your experience of a play or movie in a public theater is different than sitting at home watching the same movie on your laptop? As you bond with the hero, so does everyone else in the theater. You all laugh and cry together. You all gasp in terror and groan in disappointment as one when things go wrong. This corporate experience heightens the emotional response of each individual.

In the context of the liturgy, the communal aspect of sharing in the drama together unites us. As we join in singing, rising, standing, kneeling, and sitting together we move beyond ourselves to be united as one body. The same thing happens in the group dynamic at a dance or a sporting or political event. Our own individual cares and concerns get caught up in one another's lives. We share one another's burdens as we worship together, and just as in a play or movie the audience laughs and cries and is frightened, so at Mass we share the same experiences and thus become more closely bonded together. This is important because worship is supposed to lift us beyond ourselves to something greater. That "something greater" is the Body of Christ and the encounter with him. This is why it's not good enough to "worship God in nature" by taking a hike in the woods on Sunday or sitting on the front porch, saying a few prayers, and watching the birds.

There is one other dramatic aspect of the liturgy that is worth mentioning. Have you noticed that a drama is called a "play" and actors are called "players"? The simplest kind of drama is when children play dress-up. They raid the costume box and come out as a pirate or a princess, a buccaneer or a bride. Even when children are pretending without costumes—playing cops and robbers or cowboys and Indians—they are doing drama.

Furthermore, we all do this all the time whether we are children or not. Every day we are required to play a part and take on a role. Whether we are putting on the business suit, shirt, and tie or donning another uniform for the workplace, we are putting on a costume and playing a part. In the liturgy we take this for granted. The servers put on their cassock and surplice, the deacon his dalmatic, the priest his alb, chasuble, cincture, and stole. Some of us wear special hats too! That is all part of the drama, and it is not silly or insignificant.

When children dress up and play pretend they are stepping into a bigger part than they play in their ordinary lives. They are not really pirates or princesses, cowboys or kings, fairies or fair maidens. Likewise when the priest or deacon or altar server puts on the costume he becomes who he was ordained to be—a new man—one that is bigger than his ordinary self. The priest steps into the role of Christ the great high priest. The deacon is Christ the servant; the altar servers, the angels who wait on the throne of God.

Does this matter? I think it does. I think it matters much more than we imagine. The ordinary, down-to-earth person might sneer and think it is all a load of folderol, but why has it continued down the ages if it is no more than a vain act of mummery? We don the costumes and assume a role in the liturgy because, just as the child prepares for life by playing pretend, so we prepare for eternal life by assuming the roles that are far greater than we are, but which we will all become one day just as surely as the child one day becomes a man or a woman.

Finally, there is this: the drama of the liturgy is not only like a play, it is also like playtime. Have you ever noticed that there are some things in life that seem to be useless? What point is there, for instance, in playing football or dancing or singing? What point is there in performing a play, making a sculpture, or painting a picture? Sure, these things can be sold; some money can be made selling tickets and people may buy a program or a bag of popcorn. Sports scholarships are awarded and some people become wealthy actors, singers, or sportsmen—but that is not really why we do these things in the first place. We do them simply because they are worth doing. We do them in the same way a child plays.

Watch a child playing sometime. There are few things more joyful or more simple. A child at play is doing what he enjoys. He is doing something that he delights in. It may puzzle him and he may struggle in his game, but that too is something in which he delights. It is the same with any game, hobby, sport, or art that we enjoy. We do it for its own sake and not for money. We do it even though it is useless, and when we do these useless things we are being richly and fully human. Playtime is not meaningless.

Maybe, then, this is part of what Jesus meant when he said we must become as little children to enter the kingdom. We come in prayer, praise, and worship with the playful heart of a child. Worshiping God in simplicity and joy as a child plays.

Worship is like that. It is one of the seemingly useless things we do. Of course, in our worship we may sometimes think about doing good deeds and making the world a better place and helping poor people and becoming better ourselves, but that is not the real point of worship. If we wanted to just do that we would join the Rotary Club or the Boy Scouts, or go to a therapist, or work at the soup kitchen. No, worship is something more useless and more grand than that.

Liturgical worship is one of those beautiful things in life, like dancing, singing, painting a picture, putting on a play, or writing a poem. Through worship we not only become more human, we become more like God, because that is what God does. Rather, I should say, that is what God IS—from the very beginning we learn that he is a creator. He makes things. He makes a world. He makes a beautiful world. He makes a world that is full and abundant and alive and free.

And when he is done he rejoices and says, "Alleluia! That is good!"

8

Priests and People

DEAR MICHAEL,

I hope after my last letter you didn't tell the seminary rector that the liturgy was like going to see a Broadway play! The dramatic aspect of the liturgy can be overdone, and while I think it is important, it is also important that the liturgy does not become an overly ornate and stylized performance. It's the Holy Sacrifice of the Mass. It's not ballet.

Everything in the celebration of the liturgy should be subordinate to the action at the altar. The different elements of the celebration of the Mass play their part when they are ordered and prioritized properly. Nothing in the Mass should draw attention to itself—whether because it is very good or because it is very bad.

If Mrs. Hawkins goes out of Mass and all she says is, "Ooh, Phyllis, wasn't the choir's performance today simply divine!," then things are out of order. Likewise, if Mrs. Hawkins goes out of Mass saying, "What was the choir screeching on about this morning! It hurt my ears, and Mildred always sings out of tune!," then things are also out of order. The same applies to everything in the Mass—from the preaching to the flowers and from the altar servers to the ushers. There are proper roles and relationships for everything, and these proper roles all contribute to the overall impact of the Mass.

In the last letter I likened the liturgy to a drama, and in a play every person has their rightful part. I can remember the director of a school play telling us, "There are no small parts, only small actors." In other words, when everyone plays their rightful part the whole drama works effectively, but if anyone upstages another actor, hogs the limelight, or demands top billing they are undermining the whole production.

The way to maintain the right relationships in the liturgy is to remember the proper role each person plays. The church is ordered hierarchically, so the priest and what he does are at the top of the heap. Get it out of your mind that this is because the priest is somehow superior to everyone else. We've all known prima donna priests who like to show off and the liturgy becomes their stage.

Not good. The fact is, the priest himself doesn't matter, and any good priest will tell you that. What matters is that he is *in persona Christi capitis*. The priest is representing Christ in the order of the Mass.

We're used to the idea that the priest represents Christ in the Mass, but there is more to it than that. If the priest represents Christ, then he represents all the different aspects of Christ. He stands for Christ the Good Shepherd when he takes the part of Pastor, but he also represents Christ the Judge, Christ the King, Christ the Warrior, and Christ the Victim.

Another aspect of Christ that the priest represents can

only be understood when we see the Church as the family of God. We are all God the father's adopted children and the Church is our mother. If so, then the priest also stands for the father in the family of God.

This is the profound reason we call the priest "father" —not just because he does fatherly things like helping us and being kind and giving us guidance. The priest also performs the role of father in the family imagery, and if the father, then also the husband and the bridegroom. This connects with the nuptial imagery that runs like a golden thread throughout the sacred scriptures.

The imagery of bride and groom begins with Adam and Eve and is woven through the Old Testament: a groom is searching for his bride; God says he will come and be the husband to his bride, Israel. Time and again Jesus refers to himself as the bridegroom who comes to redeem and love his virgin bride, and St Paul picks up the image when he says that the Church is the bride of Christ. If the priest is *in persona Christi* then he not only represents Christ the priest and victim; he also represents Christ the bridegroom. This imagery is vital to the revealed nature of the Church and to God's revelation of his Son.

This is one of the profound reasons why a woman cannot be a priest. A woman might be able to represent Christ the suffering servant and victim, or Christ the shepherd and judge, but she can never represent Christ the bridegroom, husband, and father in the family of God.

It is easy for modern people to dismiss this talk as so much psycho-babble or outdated chauvinism. However, this would be to dismiss the very imagery given by God himself, from the beginning of his revelation to the world right through to the Book of Revelation. There, at the end of all things heaven is portrayed as the wedding supper of the Lamb—in other words, the reception after the wedding of Christ and his bride the Church.

I believe that this imagery, far from being old-fashioned and irrelevant, is more important today than ever before. One of the reasons our society is experiencing a breakdown in the family, gender confusion, sterility, and a crisis in that area is because we have torn up and thrown away the deeply significant symbols and signs of our humanity. The symbols of mother and father, husband and wife, parent and child are woven into the very fabric of our being, our souls, and our corporate memory. We scrub this out and scorn these things at our peril. When we break these sacred icons the curse of that action falls upon us and our children.

Finally, the image of the priest as father reaffirms and secures the rest of the powerful and profound imagery of the Church. Thus he also supports the imagery of the Christian family. When father is present with mother, the children are secure and the family is solid. When father goes the family goes. When the mother-father roles are confused, the children are confused about what it means to be a mother and father and therefore what it means to be a man or a woman.

The reason this is so easy to dismiss or overlook is that we have forgotten how this imagery works within the drama of the liturgy. Just as the royal family at a wedding represents powerful archetypes which resonate at the deepest level of the human psyche, so the priest as Father, Husband, and Bridegroom registers deeply within the human heart and affirms truths that we all know within the depth of our being.

When we remember this, everything else falls into place. The deacons are subject to the bishop, and being ordained they also serve *in persona Christi*. As such they serve the altar and the Word of God by representing Christ the suffering servant. As clergy they are robed, and function as symbols and signs of the servant nature of Christ. Images of the Blessed Virgin are prominent to the side of the priest standing at the altar because in her the love of the mother is reflected and resonates. St Joseph on the other side is another reminder of the father figure— and our belonging to the family of God.

The altar servers are robed in white because they play another function in the liturgy. They represent the angels who serve God day and night. Their function in the Mass—carrying the cross and candles or holding the book or bringing forward the gifts—is a symbol of the constant service of the angels in the court of God. This is why at the consecration altar servers should kneel before the altar of God as the angels who cry "Holy, Holy, Holy."

I was explaining this once to some altar servers in a training session, and one of their mothers was sitting in the back row of church. When I said the boys represent the angels before the throne of God she blurted out, "You gotta be kidding me!" I expect her little boy had been less than cherubic that morning.

Should you have girl altar servers? I think it is best to have only boy altar servers because their role being close to the altar is one of the ways vocations to the priesthood can be fostered. Also, it is true that boys and girls both thrive in organizations that are not co-ed. Very often if the girls become part of a typically male group the boys leave. "If the girls want to do it, they can go ahead and do it!" seems to be the attitude, and so the boys opt out.

However, the Church allows girls to be altar servers and the girls can do a fine job. They too can represent the angels before the throne of heaven. From a practical point of view, when you go to a parish where both boys and girls serve it may not be very diplomatic or pastorally smart to ban girl altar servers. Here is what I suggest: let the boys and girls serve separately. Boys serve at one Mass. Girls serve at another. Also, if you have girl altar servers, let them wear different robes so that their service and function is somewhat distinctive.

Have you ever been in one of those churches where the laypeople are extraordinary ministers of Holy Communion and they all come into the sanctuary in their street clothes, stand around the altar to receive the ciboria and chalices, then go back down to administer communion? Contrary to the rules for Mass, they return to the altar and stand around cleansing the vessels and being generally helpful. Sometimes a pastor will also load up the procession with the lay people and representatives from all the different service organizations in the parish and they all come trooping in as part of the procession, looking a bit self-conscious and awkward.

This is a shallow kind of egalitarian ideology that has crept into the liturgy. The well-meaning pastor is embarrassed by the hierarchical nature of the Church and thinks he has to destroy that by filling up the procession and the sanctuary with lots of lay people in street clothes. He thinks he is not supposed to appear superior in any way, so he compensates by getting everyone to be part of the procession. This is confusing and it not only destroys the true symbolism of the priest and people, but also makes things crowded and chaotic in the sanctuary.

The people of God should remain in their street clothes and should usually only enter the sanctuary to read the scriptures. Why? Because when they remain outside the sanctuary they actually function in a properly symbolic way in the liturgy. The role of the laity in the Church is to be out in the world proclaiming the Gospel by their ordinary lives. When they remain on the level of the nave and are dressed in their street clothes they symbolize this reality. It shows that they are the salt of the earth and the light of the world, and that they are ready to go out and be salty and radiant.

When the laity (other than altar servers) come up into the sanctuary and are given special clothes, medallions or ribbons to wear, it becomes a false attempt to include them somehow in the clerical order. This charade confuses both the specialized role of the ordained clergy and the ordinary role of the layperson in the world. Sincere people think it helps democratize the Church, but both laity and clergy are strengthened to do their work when they function in their proper places within the Church's hierarchical order. When this is explained most people understand immediately and see the beauty and truth of this symbolism.

I realize when I say "proper place" that I am a priest and it may sound like I am "putting people in their place," as if they are being uppity and need to be corrected. That is not what I mean at all. The proper place for all of us is the place of service. When Jesus washed the disciples' feet he reminded us of his words, "The greatest among you should be the servant of all." One of the pope's dearest titles is "servant of the servants of God." Therefore, when the people serve in their proper place and the priest serves in his proper place, we all see, through the symbolism of the liturgy, that self-sacrificial service is the heart of it all.

Finally, the Church and her liturgy should always be a reflection of the reality of heaven. In Dante's great masterpiece all the souls in heaven are in their proper places. Some saints surround the highest level near the throne of God. Others in that great multitude are farther down, but the great and beautiful truth is that each soul is eternally happy because each soul is exactly where it should be within the divine plan. Within the liturgy, where each person has a proper role in relationship to the priest and the action of the altar, this same dignity and humility is symbolized and experienced.

Do you think perhaps I am making too much of a fuss about this? Well, someone has to! Seriously, I think one of the great problems in our society is the constant push for recognition and a kind of false equality, and this push (ironically) is too often at the expense of other people. When we come to the liturgy, therefore, we should experience exactly the opposite. Here we experience a community of mutual service. Lay people are not clambering to be pseudo-clergy, thinking that to be up front is somewhat more special. Likewise, the priests should always remember their role as servant of the servants of God— never lording it over everyone, but serving one another in love.

If the liturgy shows this delicate and dignified dance being acted out, then the Church's worship becomes a symbol and a sign for the kind of society we ought to live in. The liturgy then becomes a sign of the kingdom of God in the world, and those who soak it up at a deep level will take that model of roles and relationships out into their homes, their workplaces, and the world.

9

Beauty:
The Language of Worship

EAR MICHAEL,

It was great to meet you and the other semi-narians last week and be able to give you a tour of the new church after Mass.

When the four of you stepped from the narthex into the nave you did what everyone does. You looked up, then you said in a hushed voice, "It's beautiful."

You might not think this is such a big deal, but it is. I first noticed this response when the church was almost finished. A couple of workmen who hadn't been on the job before stepped into the back of the church and did the same thing. They stopped. They looked up and they said in an awed voice, "It's beautiful!"

Now these guys were brawny working-class men. I think they were electricians. As far as I know they weren't Catholic. I don't even know if they had religion at all, but they still stopped, looked up, and whispered, "It's beautiful!"

This really makes me interested and excited. Why? Because there is something going on here which is very, very important for worship. You remember some time ago I wrote about language that takes us beyond language?

Well, beauty is the language that really takes us beyond language.

Here's what I mean: when people enter the back of the church they stop, look up, and say, "It's beautiful!" Do you remember that when you guys said that, I asked, "What do you think is beautiful about it?" Like everyone else you thought for a minute, looked around, and said, "Well, I like the stained glass windows," or "I don't know, I guess I like the way the light comes in." See, nobody really has words to describe their feelings beyond "It's beautiful!" We try to find other words that work, or we try to pin the feeling we've had on something particular like the windows or the statues, but the apprehension of beauty is the main thing, and it is something we don't really have enough words for.

This is why when we are really caught up in the experience of beauty we always fall silent. When you are on a mountaintop watching the sunrise you don't hang out yucking it up and yelling and talking. No. If you are in a group you are all spellbound and silent. Neither do you go into a long spiel about the pleasing effect of photons on the receptors in your eyes. You don't talk about beauty. Have you noticed how silent it is in art galleries, for instance? It is the same whenever we are in the midst of apprehending beauty. Beauty takes us beyond words into the sacred silence.

This is why it is important to build beautiful churches —because it is through the beauty that we encounter the Beautiful One—the One who is the source of all beauty and beyond all words.

There is something else I've noticed about beauty and the way it works on us: it is universal. You know how I said that people stop, look up, and whisper, "It's beautiful"? Well, that's really the response virtually everyone makes, in the same way and in the same place and with the same hushed tones. It doesn't matter if the person is a little child or a senior citizen. They might be any race, any ethnicity, or any social class. They might have a PhD in art history or they might be practically illiterate. They all stop. They look up. They all say, "It's beautiful!"

This means you do not need a degree in art to apprehend beauty. You don't even need to be able to read to apprehend beauty. Everyone gives same response to our beautiful church. This universal experience therefore recognizes a shared humanity. It brings everyone to the same level, or rather I should say it raises everyone up to a higher level of their humanity and a higher level of awareness.

This is another reason why we should take the time and trouble to build beautiful churches, because the beauty raises people up to a higher dimension of humanity, and it is at that higher level of humanity that hearts are more readily opened to the dynamic action of worship. The apprehension of beauty as we enter the church calms our soul into silence and lifts it to the realm of the beautiful.

What is really powerful about this is that it all happens naturally and un-self-consciously. Sure, we might say, "That's beautiful!," but the transaction at the depth of our being is beyond that. We open up to beauty, and as we do we also open up to truth and goodness because beauty, truth, and goodness are a little Holy Trinity. You cannot have beauty without truth and goodness. You cannot have goodness without beauty and truth and you cannot have truth without beauty and goodness. Three in one and one in three.

The apprehension of beauty I spoke about when you guys came into our new church is just the first step. In fact, beauty's being the language of worship informs everything we do in the liturgy. Yes, the church should be beautiful, but so should the music, the vestments, the readings, and the liturgical actions. I'll be writing to you about each of these things in a separate letter, but for now I'm just talking about the over-arching principles.

At college I was an art student for a couple of years, then I switched to Speech and English. I also spent a lot of time singing in choirs and performing on stage. What I learned there was that the apprehension of beauty is greatest when all the different art forms combine in one presentation. This is why I came to like opera—because acting, dance, art (in stage and costume design), vocal music, instrumental music, drama, and poetry all came together in one harmonious experience.

At least that was the theory. A lot of things went wrong, but with enough practice we made perfect... once in a while anyway!

When liturgy comes together there is also a perfect kind of experience of beauty. This experience is far greater than an opera because it is ancient and solemn and more than that—it effects what it signifies. It is a true spiritual, mental, and physical participation in what God is doing in the world.

Let me explain what I mean. When the liturgy is celebrated in a beautiful church all the art forms are meshing together in a simple, unified way. Literature is not just read by individuals from a book. It is declaimed publicly, as it has been from the beginning of time. We hear the great sagas of the Old Testament, the thunderings of the prophets, the tender, poetic words of hope in the psalms, the profound theology of St Paul, and the gripping drama of the Gospels.

The literature is integrated with vocal and instrumental music—all of which fits and illuminates the readings. In a beautiful church we are also surrounded by the beauty of art and architecture. We see the craftsmanship of metal-workers, carvers, seamstresses, painters, and sculptors in the sacred vessels, altar furniture, vestments, and art-work. When the altar servers are well trained and the clergy move together to offer the sacrifice we even see a kind of dance. When it works, all of this fits together in a harmonious unity. Each object or action has its place and purpose and all of them work in harmony, subject to the action of the Mass as it is celebrated at the altar.

Now, maybe you think this sounds too hoity-toity. Certainly if one tried to reproduce this in any other context it would be no more than an artificial aesthetic experience. Think about it: what would it be like if a group of people got together to present music interspersed with public readings from an ancient book in a specially designed building? Add the fact that they are wearing old-fashioned costumes and are re-enacting ancient rituals surrounded by other people wearing antique gear. The closest you can imagine to such an activity is perhaps a Shakespearean play.

But although it's like a play, it's not a play. It is the liturgy, and a billion ordinary people troop off to church every Sunday to participate in what might seem to many a peculiar activity. But the others rightly do so and think nothing of it. Ordinary boys with runny noses and scraped knees don robes and perform the solemn rites as men put on garments resembling the robes of ancient Romans. Quite ordinary mothers and sisters practice ancient music to sing at this ceremony while others kneel to pray and sit in silent worship.

What are they doing? They are participating in beauty, and if beauty, then truth and goodness. Furthermore, think how they are doing this. They are not booking tickets to go to a concert. They are not parking the car and going into an art gallery to look at paintings for an hour. They are not going to the theater to watch a play or going to a gallery to look at sculptures or studying a book about architecture. They are worshiping and using the building, the art, the music, and the liturgical actions in a most natural and wholesome way.

The paintings and sculpture are not standing alone in some sterile gallery. They are where they were created to be—in a niche, behind an altar or on the reredos. The people are gazing at the artwork, lighting candles, and placing flowers. They are connecting with it and participating in the art in a way no one ever does in an art gallery. Church art is not just pretty decoration. It is part of the whole act of worship.

If all of this is true, then what happens when a church is not beautiful? First we have to ask why so many modern churches are not only not beautiful but downright ugly. You can read some good books about this phenomenon, but the simple answer is that the architects and liturgists either did not understand the importance of beauty or deliberately got rid of anything beautiful because they considered it a distraction.

The reason they thought it was a distraction takes us back again to the language of worship. After the Second Vatican Council the language of the liturgy shifted from Latin to the vernacular. The Church leaders of the time were intent that everyone should be able to hear and understand the words of sacred scripture and the words of the Mass.

However, this overriding concern that everyone understand everything spawned a utilitarian or functional approach to the Mass. Not only did the people have to be able to understand; a functional approach to the Catholic faith also developed. The reason for Mass was not so much worship of Almighty God, but to get together and work for peace and justice. If the whole purpose of Mass is to encourage everyone to get busy making the world a better place, then there is no need for all that "beauty."

Furthermore, this utilitarian approach to the faith was often accompanied by what I call "fake Franciscanism." Because St Francis was poor, people made the mistake of thinking there was some virtue not only in poverty but also in everything being cheap, mass-produced, and poorly made. In fact, some people went so far as to think themselves superior because everything in their church was of poor quality. Some imagined that they were somehow more "spiritual" because they were unconcerned with physical things; but you'll remember that thinking that the physical world is inferior or doesn't matter is the old heresy of Manicheanism come back to haunt us.

I guess you can see what I'm getting at. In Catholicism everything is connected. Whether a church is beautiful or not is linked with what you think it is for and also what it *is*. To put it simply, a church should look like a church. When it does, it reveals its innate authenticity. When it does not it confuses, bewilders the viewer with a lie.

Whether a liturgy is beautiful or not is also linked with what you believe liturgy is for. If the Church is merely an organization to help the poor, and if the liturgy is just a chance to get together to hear a pep talk about how to make the world a better place, then beautiful vestments, magnificent churches, statues of saints, precious vessels, celestial music, and exquisite art are a waste of money, time, and effort. When you see it this way you can understand what the Protestant Revolution was about. They wanted to get rid of "all that fancy stuff" and worship in simplicity like Jesus and the disciples.

That sounds all well and good, but in fact Jesus and his disciples worshiped using liturgy, and the temple in Jerusalem where they went to offer sacrifice was full of "fancy stuff": golden bowls and goblets, golden altars of incense, carvings, tapestries, candlesticks, curtains, and vestments. The worship Jesus knew in the temple and synagogue was far more like traditional Catholic worship today than a Protestant megachurch with folding chairs and a big screen in a former supermarket.

What a shame that so many Catholic pastors hired architects to build big, bare barns in which to celebrate Mass. Much was lost and very little gained in such a revolution! To balance this, we should also remember that monastic orders like the Cistercians have championed an austerity in architecture and liturgy that was still beautiful in its simplicity and focus. Some of the modern churches successfully display this noble simplicity in an austere style.

Happily, we're moving away from barren barns for their own sake, and I hope you and the other seminarians will be able to see through that shallow and empty philosophy and realize why beauty is so important in worship. Quite simply, beauty is important. It is important because it moves the will toward the Good, and it fills us with delight in the work of prayer. Beauty is important because it makes apprehension of Truth a delight. Most of all, beauty is important because as we apprehend beauty we get a little glimpse of glory, a little foretaste of that heavenly country where beauty has its source and summit.

10

Images, Art, and Icons

EAR MICHAEL,

D When you and your friends came by our new church, one of the things in which you all seemed really interested was the sacred art we were able to include. I was not too pleased to hear that your seminary training includes nothing on the history of sacred art and iconography, and I was even more disappointed to learn that what instruction in art you did have was from a modern secular artist.

If this is true, it is a big gap in your training—especially as there are any number of excellent Catholic artists, architects, art history professors, iconographers, and sculptors who could help with your education. Unfortunately, a good number of priests have told me that they received no training in the history of sacred art. It was all theology, philosophy, canon law, moral theology, and more philosophy, theology, canon law and moral theology.

The history of sacred art is fascinating, and you'll remember from my letter about beauty being the language of worship that the interaction we have with art and architecture is a vital part of Catholic worship. It's important because our faith is incarnational and sacramental. The physical things matter. For Christians matter matters because God's Son himself took on human flesh in place and time. Since he is the image of the unseen God, images are important.

What is the point of art in churches? Too often the members of well-meaning building committees treat Catholic sacred art like they treat the decor in their homes. They build a church, then they decide they had better have some statues and pictures; and so they go to a church catalog and buy some stuff that everybody likes and that has a cheap price tag. Then they plonk it down somewhere in church and put a candle stand in front of it.

Well, maybe... but not quite. In fact, the art in a church building should complement and refer back to the sacrifice of the Mass and therefore, like everything else in the church and the liturgy, should be subordinate to the altar. If the object of the liturgy is worship, the question becomes, "How does the art in our churches aid worship?"

The first thing to consider is the style of art. What about modern abstract art? Shouldn't a modern church feature modern art? First we should distinguish between modern art and contemporary art. Because the art is produced today doesn't mean it is "modern." So let's use the term "modernist" art. Should a modern church feature modernist art?

I don't think so, and here's why. Firstly, most modernist artists are trying to make a statement of originality. There is nothing wrong with originality, but originality is not the sole criterion for good art. Too often the modernist artist, in trying to be original, values *only* originality, and by originality he means being subversive, rebellious, and iconoclastic. There is a kind of arrogance in this approach, and therefore it is difficult for modern art to be subordinate to the architecture of the whole church and subordinate to the altar. Modern art too often tries to "make a statement." Even if that statement is Christian in intent, the art (like the artist) is too often just being preachy and drawing attention to itself.

There is a modern Madonna in the new cathedral in Los Angeles that is a good example of this. When you see her you are disturbed, but you're not sure why. Then you learn that the artist designed the Madonna to have the features of every different racial group. This was an attempt to show that the Blessed Virgin was the mother of all Christians. It was, perhaps a clever idea, but the artist had never heard that quip by Ogden Nash, "Here is a good rule of thumb: Too clever is dumb." The result is a statue of the Blessed Virgin that might make the artist's preachy point, but the image of the Blessed Mother is not warm, maternal, and welcoming, but a kind of disconcerting alien being.

It is also true that much modernist art is asymmetrical and dissonant on purpose. How can art that is full of conflict and lacking in harmony be part of the worship of a God of symmetry, harmony, and peace?

Modernist art is also most often abstract, and while much church decoration is abstract, like tile work and some stained glass, I think it is almost impossible for Christian art to be purely abstract. Here's why: because

109

Jesus Christ is true God and true Man. He is not an abstraction. God's action in history is always real and fleshed out. Jesus as a vague abstraction is a gnostic concept. Jesus, Mary, and the saints are real people from a real place and time who have been transformed by God's grace. Therefore, portrayals of them and their lives in an abstract way simply don't work. It is not a portrayal. It's a betrayal.

What's bad about sacred art that is abstract? To be perfectly frank, it is usually bad not only because modernist artists often understand nothing about the history of sacred iconography, but also because they do not accept the need for the artwork to be subordinate to the action of the Mass and they do not understand the intricate problems of Christian art. They do not understand how the Catholic artist is submissive to the great tradition. The sacred (as opposed to the secular) artist is operating within a two-thousand-year-old stream of experience, spirituality, and worship.

Part of that tradition is the understanding that the sacred image is a secondary image of Jesus Christ who is "the image of the unseen God" (Col. 1:5). The saints are reflections of Jesus in the world, and images of the saints therefore need to capture the mystery of the incarnation. Therefore, the Catholic artist has a special challenge when he portrays a sacred scene and saints. He has to make the saints realistic enough to be recognizable as ordinary people, but he also has to portray them as having been transformed by grace into divinized people. He or she has to portray the saint as both ordinary and extraordinary at the same time. That's not easy. If you go too far toward realism you end up with a Norman Rockwell type of picture. If you go too far toward "holiness" the figure seems spooky, strange, and otherworldly. This is why it is best to stay with traditional styles: because the successful sacred artist knows how to work within the tradition and face this unique challenge. Furthermore, his audience is likely to be familiar with the language of the icon or the traditional Catholic image.

Because of this inner humility the chances are greater that the icon will do what it is supposed to do—be a window through which we gaze, not a painting or sculpture we look at for its own sake.

To produce art within the great tradition does not mean every statue, picture, icon, or mosaic in a church has to be a dull copy of a Catholic masterpiece. A good artist knows how to be creative within the great tradition, yet still produce an original work of art that is beautiful and true. A good artist does so as a poet writes a sonnet. The tradition provides the structure for his creativity to blossom. For an inferior artist the structure confines and limits him.

If you get the chance to build or renovate a church you may have the opportunity to commission some sacred art. There are some fine young Catholic artists who would be eager to hear from you! A search through the New Liturgical Movement website will put you in touch with some of them.

Does this mean every piece of art in church has to be an expensive original commission from a living artist? I don't think so. In our new church we combined some new commissions with some fine work purchased from church catalogs as well as antique mosaics, statues, and altar ware we found from various church salvage companies. The mixture in our church is, therefore, antiques, new mass-produced work, and contemporary original commissions.

If you do get to build or renovate a church, you should take the opportunity to think things through carefully and get professional advice. The art, decoration, and images of the saints should all be part of a well-thought-out program that reflects the hierarchical nature of the Church and the priority of the sacrifice of the Mass. Pride of place therefore goes to the altar, the main crucifix, and the area of the sanctuary. While the crucifix is primary, a secondary image referring to the sacrifice or kingship of Christ can also be featured. So on the front of the altar there might be a portrayal of the *Agnus Dei*—the Lamb of God—and in the apse there might be a fresco of the Lord enthroned in glory.

I will say more about the layout of the sanctuary area and the church itself in another letter, but what about other images of saints? They should reflect the hierarchy of heaven in both their placement and their significance. So the primary images of the Mother of God and of St Joseph should be at the front, in the secondary position after the altar and crucifix.

Other statues of saints should be placed elsewhere

according to their importance. Generally speaking there should not be more than one dominant image of the Blessed Mother and Our Lord. If the faithful wish for an image of the Divine Mercy, the Sacred Heart of Jesus, or a favorite image of the Virgin Mary other than the primary image, these should be placed elsewhere in the church—creating special shrines in the narthex or some other meeting place.

What about style? As you study the history of sacred art you come to understand how the different styles of art reflect not only the different periods of church history, but the philosophy, theology, and culture of each period. The art you choose for your church should be consistent with the architecture of the church, and the various works of art should connect and fit with each other. So, for example, if your church is Gothic, the art should be fitting. Everything does not have to match perfectly. There is room for different styles within reason. However, to put a piece of harsh, modern art in a Gothic church is unreasonable, and calls attention to itself. Likewise, to place a Baroque painting with an ornate gilded frame in a modern church is jarring and incongruous.

I will say more about this when I write about architecture, but when you are choosing art for a church building the main thing to remember is that it should not draw attention to itself. Its function is to inspire devotion and lift the worshiper's heart and mind to heaven. Sacred art is like a telescope—it is something you look through to better glimpse the heavens. If the artwork draws attention to itself because it is either magnificent or magnificently ugly, it has missed the target.

I should also remind you about the question of quality and originality. Our technological age allows for the reproduction of masterpiece paintings. Don't use prints of famous paintings. Why not? For one reason, they are fake and cheap and they look it. They don't stand up to the test of time because they fade, crack, and decay quickly. But more than that, these famous art pieces have become bland and uninspiring to most people. They have seen Michelangelo's Pietà, Leonardo's Last Supper, and Madonnas by Raphael so frequently that these have lost their impact. They have some use for private devotions, but in the church itself it is better not to have them on display at all.

If the image of a saint is going to be displayed, remember that this is for Catholic devotion, not Catholic decoration. Decide which saints you and your people want to honor, then invest in a good statue, painting, or icon. You'd be surprised how affordable they are if you shop around. Look into some of the companies that salvage church antiques or some of the artists who are eager for a commission to do original work. Remember, it is better to have a few good items than a church full of junk.

A good painting or work of art might cost thousands of dollars, but that cost spread out over a hundred years of its lifetime in a church is negligible. Your people will love to be involved in this kind of project and will donate the finances, time, and energy to make their church beautiful.

Finally, you should understand how art works on the imagination to inspire worship and prayer. This happens in two ways. First, there is a general apprehension of beauty. We see something and are drawn to its natural beauty without giving it much thought. When we apprehend beauty in stained glass windows, statues, flowers, paintings, or beautiful architecture we are connecting wordlessly with God who is Beauty itself. The atmosphere of heightened beauty in a church produces higher thoughts, dreams, and resolutions. A generally beautiful environment contributes to beautiful behavior.

I have seen this in a practical way in our new church. The beauty and dignity of the building and the art have led to better behavior in church. People are less likely to come to church dressed badly. They are less likely to whisper and talk in church, and they are more likely to spend time after their prayers simply gazing around to appreciate the beauty of God's temple.

There is a second way that beauty touches us, and this has more to do with that sub-linguistic level of our being. Do you remember how I spoke about the symbolic effect of the priest, the deacon, and the servers? The role they play resonates symbolically in the depths of our mind and heart.

The same is true with the imagery in the church. The statue of Mary connects with all our deep feelings of the Mother. A statue of a virgin martyr like St Maria Goretti or a virgin like St Thérèse of Lisieux opens us up to the feelings not only about that saint, but about childhood, innocence, the crimes of violence, and the suffering of Christ's body. St Joseph unfolds masculinity, fatherhood, justice, and chastity. The image of someone like St Benedict with his long beard and aged appearance unlocks in our minds and hearts all our thoughts and emotions about grandfathers, and the wisdom of old mentors and guides. This power of art to connect with archetypes and unlock the deepest reservoirs within our mind and heart should not be neglected, and therefore the care and thought you use in placing these images should reflect their power and the graces God pours through them.

There is much more that can be said about art in churches, but that's for you to discover. I encourage you to take an interest in church art and architecture. Don't treat it as a sideline. Be enthusiastic to learn about the history. Learn about the great painters and sculptors and architects. Learn about the development of the various types of architecture and the different crafts and skills of painting, mosaics, ceramics, carving, and decoration. Remember that beauty is the language of worship. While these things are not the most important, they are very important.

11

Temples or Auditoriums?

EAR MICHAEL,

I can't help it. I travel around America visiting various churches and it is hard for me to be polite about the church buildings. I know. I know. I'm spoiled. I lived in England for twenty-five years. I was blessed to travel around Europe and visit some of the most fantastic churches, cathedrals, and abbeys.

For two years I was chaplain at King's College Cambridge—one of the most sublime buildings in Christendom. I used to make my annual retreat at the amazing abbey of Mont Saint-Michel in France. I fell in love with the grand cathedrals of England, the homely village churches, the great abbeys of France, and the glorious churches of Rome, Florence, and Siena.

I'm spoiled.

Then when I returned to the United States I found that Modernism in architecture was everywhere. For all their claims of originality and novelty, the suburban churches were remarkably bland, unimaginative, and uniformly ugly. When I would visit these parishes I made it a point to ask the people if they liked their church building. Usually they would pause, looking for a way to be polite, and they would say something like, "You know I really like the padded pews," or "the sound system works really well. You can hear everything." What they never said was that the church was beautiful or that it was an inspiring place in which to worship.

The fan-shaped churches that became so popular in American suburbs in the seventies and eighties were the result of the new emphasis on the Eucharist as sacred feast rather than sacrifice. If the Mass was a sacred fellowship meal, then it was understandable that the church should be round so that as many people as possible could gather around the family table.

Along with the shift in emphasis toward the people of God rather than God himself came a certain kind of American egalitarianism. Embarrassed by the hierarchical nature of the Church, pastors and liturgists stressed the equality of the people of God. This ideology also dictated that everyone sit, as much as possible, on the same level. Kneelers went out because it was considered degrading to kneel. Instead communion was to be received standing, and in the hand.

Along with these objectives, a utilitarian approach to church architecture became the norm. If Mass is not so much about worship as about being agents for change in society, then practicality is the most important thing, and this approach influenced church architecture. Was the new church comfortable? Could everyone hear and see? Were there good restrooms? A cry room? A bride's room? Most of all, was the new building affordable? "Beautiful" became another word for "expensive," so the buildings were constructed cheaply, often from inferior materials and with poor craftsmanship.

Most of all, the ugly modern churches were not only built with no apparent knowledge of the great tradition of Catholic architecture, but sometimes the architects and liturgists designed with an intent to subvert and destroy the great tradition. Everything was to be original in this brave new world after the revolutionary Second Vatican Council. But what they gained in functionality and comfort they lost in any sense of beauty, transcendence, and rootedness in the great tradition.

The modern, round suburban churches of the United States also lacked any Catholic distinctiveness. This fit the ecumenical spirit of the age. It seemed that Catholics and Protestants were about to be united. If the church buildings all looked alike, and the Catholic churches were rid of all those statues and candles and stained glass windows, they would be able to blend with the Protestants more easily.

Now that I've gone on a little rant, it has to be admitted that many of the churches before the Second Vatican Council also left much to be desired. They were not all glorious Gothic masterpieces. Many were extremely ugly in their own way. They were often dark and dingy, or fallen into disrepair. Too often they were huge drafty barns where people could not see and hear.

You can see why a new generation wanted something better, something newer, something built for the new spirit of the age in which God's people would be able to worship in full participation—hearing the Word of God and connecting with the action of the Mass. The large round churches seemed to be exactly what was needed, and sincere liturgists and pastors pushed through the architectural reforms they were so sure were needed.

I get pretty passionate about this, Michael, but I'm also aware that it is not quite so easy as saying, "Let's just build old-fashioned beautiful churches again." The fact of the matter is that the Second Vatican Council has happened and there are many good things that have come from it. It is better that the people should be able to hear what is going on at Mass. It is better that there should be a higher level of participation. It is better that the people are consciously involved, and the church building is an important part of that process.

You and your fellow seminarians will be charged with building new churches and renovating old ones. It is necessary, therefore, to keep all these principles in mind. How do we build new churches that are within the great tradition of Catholic architecture but still have the functionality and purpose we need in post-Vatican II worship? Do we simply build big auditoriums but add a few fake Gothic arches or pop in a few stained glass windows? That seems to be the solution in many of the more recently built Catholic churches. They are certainly better than the 1970s and '80s buildings, but these "Gothic auditoriums" lack authenticity. Their "churchiness" seems to be pasted on as an afterthought, no more than a superficial decoration. This latest generation of auditorium churches are "churchy" in the way an Italian restauranteur creates atmosphere by erecting plastic pillars and putting empty wine bottles, plastic grapes, and pictures of Rome around the place.

Where do we go to find the principles of church architecture that are modern and accessible and yet also part of the great tradition? I think we'll find the answer in the Bible. Imagine that! The fact of the matter is that God outlined some plans for a proper place of worship. The details are found in the Books of Exodus and Leviticus, where Moses is instructed to build the tabernacle—the traveling temple the Jews used in their desert wanderings. That same model was used when Solomon and Herod built the temples in Jerusalem.

Does this mean we should build little replicas of the Jerusalem Temple? Of course not—but what we can gather is that first of all, God gave a plan for church architecture. Second, He gave a plan for a temple, not an auditorium or lecture hall. Third, He gave a plan for a place of sacrifice. If the liturgy is first and foremost the offering of the divine sacrifice, then we ought to pay attention to the plan God laid out in the Bible for a temple where sacrifice is offered.

That plan is very simple. It has three parts: an outer court for the people, a holy place where the sacrifices are offered, and a Holy of Holies which is the dwelling place of God. In fact, from the earliest times and in every place until the modern age, most Catholic churches (with few exceptions) followed this plan. The church was basically rectangular. In the main section, the nave, the people stood or sat. The sanctuary (also called the chancel) was the place where the sacrifice of the Mass was offered, and beyond that was the Holy of Holies—the tabernacle where the sacrament was reposed. This basic structure varied somewhat in various places, but the essential three divisions remained the same.

This structure was not only practical, but it also emphasized two important aspects of Christian theology. First of all, it was linear. In other words, with the rectangular shape it had a beginning and an end—an Alpha point and an Omega point. A round church does not have this linear aspect in the same way. Does it matter? It does, because the Christian view of history is linear. It has a beginning point and an end point. Pagan cosmologies are circular. They emphasize the cycle of life, re-incarnation, and a spiral of existence.

The second point about the classical structure of the church is that it was hierarchical. There was a step-by-step progression from people to clergy to the dwelling place of the presence of God. The hierarchical aspect was not so much to place the clergy above the people because they are superior, but because the clergy offer the sacrifice that is the bridge to God and the mediating action between God and the people. A hierarchical church visualizes a stairway to heaven, or a ladder of ascent.

I would add a third point about traditional churches that comes not from the Jewish tabernacle model, but from the Catholic tradition: that the church has verticality. It has height. When you come in you immediately want to look up. This verticality is the hallmark of all the greatest Catholic churches, and the height of the building therefore lifts the soul as it lifts the eyes; the lift in our hearts reminds us that in worship we aspire to rise from this world to the heights of heaven. In the Mass we say, "Lift up your hearts," and a tall church gives those words symbolic strength.

Can a modern church be designed to incorporate this ancient model while still accommodating the good aspects of the Second Vatican Council? I think it can. One tradition that developed in the Middle Ages is the cruciform (cross-shaped) church. Transepts extended out on either side from the basic rectangle. A cruciform church with transepts can accommodate a good number of people, and if the sanctuary or holy place is moved forward into the crossing where the transepts and nave meet, more people can be seated where they can see and hear the action of the Mass adequately.

What about affordability? Modern architects are quick to tell building committees that they cannot afford a traditional church. It is true that if they wish to build out of cut limestone or solid brick with hand-carved stone pillars the cost is prohibitive, but with modern technologies and new materials and techniques a traditional church is just as affordable as a modern structure.

You have seen the new church we built in Greenville. It is a beautiful Romanesque-style building, but it was very affordable. We built it for less than half of what many architects predicted. This is because we were not ashamed to use steel construction methods, modern materials, and new techniques to replicate the old style of building.

Some architects get a little bit snooty and say, "Yes, we can build in a traditional style, but those buildings are just fake old buildings. They're just a copy of an out-of-date style. To be authentic we must build in a modern style for modern people." I disagree. Older styles like the Romanesque and Gothic are, like the Catholic faith itself, ever ancient and ever new.

A church built in an older style helps Catholics live within the great tradition. But can a new church be modern in design—not just a replica Gothic or Romanesque church? I think so. If the church is designed with an understanding of sacramental authenticity and purpose the style will take care of itself. There are some good examples of modern churches that have three sections, linear form, and vertical height, and the ones that are well built from good materials are beautiful buildings for worship—not because they are modern or ancient, but because they follow some simple principles of beauty in church architecture.

With all this in mind, you may not get the chance to build a new church. You will, however, probably have the chance to renovate an old church. There are two distinct kinds of challenges here. The first is to renovate a genuinely old church that was remodeled badly in the '70s or '80s. A good designer or architect who is sympathetic to your cause will help you bring that old church back to its former glory while also bringing it up-to-date, keeping in mind the great tradition and the demands of modern worship.

The second challenge will be to renovate one of the flat, round churches from the 1970s or '80s. Many of these churches are now run-down and in need of renovation anyway. If the building is poorly built from cheap materials, be bold and begin with a bulldozer! However, if the parish is not ready to tear it down and build a new traditionally-styled church, it is often possible to incorporate traditional elements into the modern buildings in a sympathetic way. Again, a good architect will be able to guide you on the best way to integrate traditional elements—not only as decoration or in some artificial attempt to make the modern church look old-fashioned, but because the modern church can be modified to provide the best environment for truly reverent liturgy. The aim here is not to clutter up a modern building with antiques, but to adapt the modern building according to the principles I have outlined.

Sometimes a modern church building can be altered simply and effectively with the smart use of lighting. Instead of the typical lighting plan where everything is bright and uniform, a professional and subtle lighting plan can de-emphasize the worst parts of the building and neutralize them while accentuating the altar and shrines of saints, bringing the focus of the people where it should be.

Don't imagine you can do it yourself. Hire a professional. A good designer who understands the principles of traditional worship might introduce a baldacchino into a vast open space in a large church. This traditional canopy over the altar brings the focus toward the altar, where it should be. It could be that a newly designed retable can be placed at the east end and the tabernacle moved to a central position in order to salvage the space for more reverent worship. If the altar is a modern wooden table, replace it with a traditionally designed altar, and if you can't afford that, cover it with an altar frontal and introduce candles and a crucifix that are in keeping with the tradition.

Whatever is done needs to be done thoughtfully, in accord with the principle that the church is a temple—the dwelling place of the Lord. Therefore we build "out" from the altar and tabernacle. Decorations or traditional elements are not added just for effect, but so that the attention might be drawn to the altar and tabernacle—transforming what was a bare auditorium into a temple where the people come into the house of the Lord to worship.

12

Turning
Toward the Lord

EAR MICHAEL,

D   Do you remember the tempest in the teapot some time ago when Cardinal Sarah instructed some priests to celebrate Mass *ad orientem*—facing the same direction as the people? Conservative Catholics rejoiced and liberal Catholics were horrified. Various bishops instructed their clergy not to turn their back to the people while others liberated their priests to do just that. Finally Pope Francis stepped in and said that there was not going to be any imminent change in the widespread practice of the priest celebrating Mass facing the people.

I expect your professors have connected you with the most important book on this subject. It is by Fr Uwe Michael Lang and is called *Turning Towards the Lord*. Fr Lang has done extensive research on the history of this question and all the pros and cons regarding whether we should face the people as we celebrate Mass or pray in the same direction as the people.

You'll know by now that *ad orientem* means "toward the east" and is the form of celebrating the Mass in which the priest stands at the altar praying in the same direction as the people. *Versus populum* celebration means "toward the people" or facing the people. *Ad orientem* was the position of the priest for the vast majority of time and in most places down the ages. After the Second Vatican Council, *versus populum* celebration swept through the Church almost overnight. Despite the fact that it was never mandated, most priests simply started to face the people. In fact, when you read the rubrics of the Mass closely you'll see that it is assumed that the priest is facing the same direction as the people to celebrate Mass. Otherwise, why would we have the instruction at *"Behold the Lamb of God"* for the priest to "face the people"? He can't really turn to face the people if he is already facing them!

It is not for me, in a short chapter, to argue the advantages of *ad orientem* celebration of the Mass. Fr Lang does that most convincingly in his book. Instead I'd like to think about the advantages and disadvantages from a pastoral point of view, then give some practical advice.

First of all, it can be difficult to introduce *ad orientem* celebration of Mass without the people grumbling "why is Father turning his back to us?" It must be admitted that *versus populum* celebration has the advantage that the people can not only see the priest but also see what he is doing and participate more fully in the action at the altar. If our criterion is that the people should focus on the offering of the sacrifice of the Mass, then it would make sense that this is better done if they are able to see what is going on.

This is countered, however, by a very important theological point. The offering of the sacrifice is Christ's offering to the Father. The priest and the people as the Body of Christ make this offering. Therefore this unanimous action should have both priest and people facing toward the Lord together.

There is a further practical consideration. When I am celebrating Mass in the *ad orientem* position, I feel not only that I am praying with the people facing the Lord, but that they are supporting me and behind me in prayer. I feel much more like I am leading them in worship and that we are one. When I am praying in the same direction as the people I also feel that my attention is toward the Lord and not toward the people. It really does feel like we are facing the Lord together, unified in our prayer.

While this is the effect for the priest, a similar thing happens for the people. They take their eyes off the priest and focus instead on the Lord. When I face the people it is very difficult to forget myself. The psychology of body language is such that I feel like I am "on show" and that I have to "make this meaningful for everyone." Despite my best intentions to focus only on what is happening at the altar, I am aware that all eyes are on me, and quite honestly, I wish they weren't. I wish they were on the Lord. If I am *in persona Christi* as the priest, that is when I want the people not to look at me but to look through me.

In all Catholic churches a crucifix is supposed to be displayed prominently by the altar. Ideally, it is above the altar or high on the east wall. When this is the case, and the people can only see the priest's back, they must look somewhere, and they are far more likely to gaze on the crucifix. This is the primary reason why I favor *ad orientem* celebration of Mass—because, as St Paul says, "We preach Christ and him crucified." And "Not me, but Christ lives in me." In other words, with *ad orientem* prayer the people look beyond the priest to Christ crucified, and that brings the proper priority and focus to the celebration of Mass.

When the priest faces the people, on the other hand, the body language of the priest and the people is circular and therefore self-centered. In a round church with everyone seated around the altar, and with the priest facing the people, the entire dialogue is circular. While the attention is rightly toward the altar and the action on the altar, as long as the dialogue is circular the attention of the worshipers cannot go beyond the altar.

There are a couple of other aspects to *ad orientem* worship worth considering. When we worship toward the east we are facing the rising sun, and an early tradition developed in which the rising sun was a daily reminder of the rising Son—that is, the Son of God. So churches were built facing east. With windows in the eastern wall, the morning sun flooded into the church and onto the altar where, on Sunday morning, the resurrection of the Son of God was being celebrated.

Furthermore, in Western Europe, to face east was also to face Jerusalem. Jerusalem was the symbol of the soul's destination, the city of God, the capital of our true country. Jerusalem the Golden was the city of the glorious East, the city of David, the site of our Lord's Passion and

Resurrection; to face Jerusalem was to turn our hearts homing.

Because of this symbolism, facing east to celebrate the Mass contributes to the transcendental atmosphere of worship. Rather than a circular focus on us and our little local community, we are facing together toward God, toward the rising sun, toward Jerusalem the earthly symbol of our heavenly home.

If we were all to return to *ad orientem* worship I am convinced that we would have far fewer difficulties with priests trying to put on a good show. Priests would disappear more; their own personalities would not intrude quite so much. This is important to remember because the liturgy is not the effort of any one individual. It is not Fr Fabulous's Mass, and it is not even the Mass at St Gabriel's. Nor is it the Mass of the people of the parish. It is the Mass of the whole Church of Christ triumphant down the ages.

All that being said, for pastoral reasons it is rarely easy to introduce *ad orientem* worship. The first thing that needs to be done is extensive catechesis. When it was introduced at a parish where I was working, the pastor took six weeks to explain what was happening and why. Then the change was introduced gradually. Once it was explained, the people accepted the change and now most of the parishioners would not want to go back to *versus populum* celebration. They have said to me, "This new way feels more reverent." Or "I'm glad I don't have to look at the pastor . . . but don't take that the wrong way!"

In some dioceses *ad orientem* worship is forbidden, and in some parishes it simply isn't pastorally sensitive to introduce the change for a whole range of reasons. When that it the case, there are still some things a priest can do to orient the worship away from himself and away from the people toward the Lord.

Firstly he can make sure there is a large crucifix placed prominently in the church near the altar. Secondly, he can make sure the tabernacle—the focus of the Lord's sacramental presence—is not in a side chapel, but placed centrally and visible. Thirdly, he can make sure the altar IS an altar and not an insignificant table. These visual elements all help to draw attention to the sacrifice of the Mass and away from the idea of a family meal at which the priest is the presiding host.

Within the celebration of the liturgy some things can also be done to orient the worship toward the Lord. In the procession, the priest and deacon should venerate the altar facing the Lord. After venerating the altar they can stand facing east for a moment of silent prayer. This begins the liturgy with a moment of shared east-facing prayer.

During the opening rite the priest can turn to face east with the people as together they say the penitential prayers. He and the servers and deacons can also turn to the east and pray in the same direction of the people during the prayers of the faithful. When the gifts are brought forward the priest can again stand reverently for a moment in silent prayer before the altar facing east. After the ablutions, as the priest says, "Pray, brothers and sisters...," the altar servers should process to places in front of the altar where they kneel facing east. This also orients the prayers of the people toward the Lord.

Even if the priest does not celebrate the Mass facing the same direction as the people, there is a time of adoration just after the sharing of the Peace and before the invitation, "Behold the Lamb of God..." As the people are sharing the peace, the priest could walk to the front of the altar and, after the sharing of the Peace is concluded, join the people in kneeling in adoration before the invitation is given, facing the same direction as they are before standing to take the chalice and paten and (observing the rubrics at that point) turn to face the people saying, "Behold the Lamb of God Who takes away the sins of the world."

After Communion, as the priest turns to repose the sacrament in the tabernacle, he has another opportunity to remain facing east. After reposing the sacrament and genuflecting he can remain facing east again for a moment of prayer. Likewise, before the closing prayer he can turn east for a moment of silence. All of these actions help to turn the direction of prayer eastward even though the celebration may still be facing the people.

In short, while celebrating the Mass the priest should visibly speak to the people at the points in the Mass when he is supposed to be addressing them, and he should focus on the actions of the altar and lifting his eyes to heaven to the Lord when that is his proper focus. If the priest looks at the people the whole time he is praying, and if he is always speaking in tones as if he is addressing the people, the whole action of the Mass is subverted and the attention is turned away from God to the people, rather than directing their attention away from the priest and away from themselves toward the Lord.

Finally, the altar servers, readers, extraordinary ministers of holy communion, and all the people should be reminded regularly of the presence of the Lord in the tabernacle. A centrally placed tabernacle should be reverenced carefully, thus reminding everyone of the orientation of prayer toward the Lord together.

13

In Vestments Veritas

Dear Michael,

Have you come across the English biblical scholar Margaret Barker? She's an extraordinary woman—a Methodist amateur scholar who's come up with some amazing research and insights. I corresponded with her when my book about the Magi was in the works. She very kindly read the manuscript and we got talking about shared interests.

One of her pet projects is discovering information about the Hebrew religion before the destruction of Jerusalem by Nebuchadnezzar in 586 BC. She's unlocked lots of details about "first temple" Judaism, and one of the things I found most interesting was the intricate theological symbolism of the temple.

I wrote about the importance of symbolism, and how it connects our subconscious and conscious minds and also connects through the imagination to our shared memories and consciousness as human beings. I don't have time to go into all of Margaret Barker's findings about the Temple, but a few of them show how much our Catholic traditions are in continuity with the worship of the Hebrews so long ago.

Here's just one example. Maybe you are familiar with

the menorah—the seven-branch candlestick in the Jewish Temple? The seven lamps on the menorah stood for the seven days of creation and the seven known planets. Then the Catholic tradition of having six candles on the altar—and the sanctuary lamp as the seventh—made sense. The seven lamps could be seen as the Catholic version of the menorah. The number seven was significant and also connected with the seven spirits of God, and the seven seals and seven bowls of judgment in the Book of Revelation. Anyway—you should read Barker. It is really fascinating stuff.

I mention her research because it gives meaning to much of the symbolism in Catholic worship—including the vestments we wear—but before I talk about her discoveries, stop for a moment to ask why we wear the vestments at all. When you read the history of the development of the vestments some scholars say they were at first simply the formal dress of Roman noblemen. Think of wearing a tuxedo or your best suit. That's all the dalmatic and chasuble were at first. The cope? That's just a fancy version of a cloak first worn to keep warm in freezing monasteries and during outdoor processions in dreary weather. So why did these special "ordinary" clothes develop into specialized clerical vestments?

Protestants might say, "Come now, all this symbolism you claim for these vestments is a lot of fanciful nonsense. They were the ordinary street clothes of ancient Romans and you have made them into the sacred vestments of a hierarchical priesthood. Why not come down to earth and wear ordinary clothes to church? Why must you dress up in all the silk, embroidery, brocade, and lace?"

Maybe they have a point, but I'm always wary of the "merely" mentality. The merely mentality reduces everything to what is useful, cuts away all that at first seems superfluous, and through a kind of harsh utilitarianism eliminates all that is thought ornate, elaborate, or artificial. But think how barren life would be if we applied that principle to everything. Instead of nice meals we'd take a nutrition pill. Instead of nice clothes we'd wear overalls or boiler suits. Instead of nice china and cutlery we'd eat every meal off paper plates with a plastic spoon. Life would be very barren indeed.

As the Mass became more ceremonial and symbolic it was natural for things to become more beautiful, in the same way that it is natural to dress up for a royal event or a wedding and to have a beautiful meal and celebration for the reception. After all, the Mass is a foretaste of a royal wedding—the marriage supper of the Lamb—the glory of all things. That it is celebrated with noble beauty is nothing to apologize for.

As this developed it was also natural for the clothing the priests wore to take on a sacred significance. The sacred garments of the priest were not only beautiful, but they also hearkened back to the Jewish priesthood, which was blessed with sacred vestments. This movement from ordinary clothing to liturgical vestments happens naturally—and not only for Catholics. In his classic book *The Shape of the Liturgy*, Dom Gregory Dix tells the story of how English Baptist preachers wore frock coats to church when a frock coat was the simple formal wear of an English gentleman. When frock coats went out of style the Baptist preacher still wore his to church and called it his "preaching coat." What had been an ordinary garment became a sacred vestment—even for a Baptist!

So we have an instinct to dress our clergy in vestments. Why is that? I think it is because any kind of a uniform blanks out the person's personality and raises his identity to a general and corporate level. When I put on the vestments it's not Dwight anymore. It's not even Father Dwight. It's the priest ready to offer the sacrifice that is the worship of the whole Church.

What's the meaning of the vestments? There's actually a deeper theological symbolism at work too. Margaret Barker explains that in the Jewish temple there was a great veil or curtain between the Holy Place or sanctuary in the temple—where the sacrifices were offered—and the Holy of Holies. The Holy of Holies was the inner room, empty except for the Ark of the Covenant, which was deemed to be the throne of God.

Once a year the high priest would go in to the Holy of Holies to compete certain prayers and ceremonies. Then he would come from the invisible God's presence in the Holy of Holies back to the sanctuary. This would happen in the sight of the people who were gathered for this solemn rite. Now here is where it gets interesting: the veil of the temple was woven from white linen and wool of three different colors: blue, purple, and red. These four colors represented the four basic elements of the physical realm—earth, air, fire, and water. Red was for fire. Blue was for air. Purple was for water because the dye to produce the purple yarn was taken from the gland of a mollusk in the sea. The white stood for the earth because it was the color of the linen which grew in the earth. These four colors, when woven together, symbolized the whole physical realm of creation. Therefore the veil symbolized the material world.

The priest's vestments were also made from cloth woven from these same four elements. Why did they go to such lengths to produce the veil and the priest's garments? Was it just to make things pretty and have some decoration? Hardly. There was a symbolic meaning to every detail in the temple. The key here lies in the ceremony of the priest going in to the Holy of Holies and emerging again. What was significant was not his going *in* to the Holy of Holies, but his emerging *from* it.

When the High Priest emerged from the presence of the Lord, he came through the veil, which represented the physical realm, and he wore vestments woven with the same colors to symbolize the physical realm. Therefore the entire ceremony symbolized the incarnation— when God's own son would come from the invisible realm into this world and would do so by taking human flesh, or putting on the physical realm. Suddenly I understood the line from that hymn *Alleluia, Sing to Jesus*: "Robed in flesh, the Great High Priest, Thou [Jesus] on earth both priest and victim in the Eucharistic Feast."

Jesus was robed in flesh, and that is the true significance of the vestments we wear to celebrate Mass. The white alb represents our baptismal regeneration and purity, and the different-colored vestments symbolize the physical realm and therefore Christ—the great high priest who was robed in flesh.

What really made me sit up and notice is that in the Catholic Church today we do not have one vestment woven from four colors, but we do have vestments of four different colors worn for different seasons of the year, and the four colors are almost the same as those in the Old Testament: white, red, purple, and green (evolved from the original blue). Knowing this, when I recently had to commission a set of vestments for our new church I asked that the green chasubles have a deep blue lining, in memory of the original four colors used in Hebrew worship.

A Protestant friend asked me once, "Why do you have to wear all those robes for your worship service? Why is it so important?" This indicates one of those clear divides between the Catholic and Protestant mentalities. We use vestments in worship because our faith is symbolic and sacramental. We use these visible, physical things to evoke and connect with the invisible realities they represent. We also wear them because their beauty shows the beauty of the glorified Christ who is clothed in the majesty and beauty of the whole created order.

It is the same with all the physical aspects of our worship. The symbolism is profound, and it takes us right back not only to the roots of Catholic worship over the last two thousand years, but also into our shared roots of worship with the Hebrews, and further into the shared customs and worship practices of our fellow human beings in other religions. There are certain symbols and customs that are so universal that they must connect deeply with our shared consciousness and human memory.

So, for example, we use incense in worship. We light candles. We place flowers. We use holy water to bless ourselves. We make artwork and statues of our beloved saints. We make the sign of the cross. We bow and genuflect. We kneel to pray. We build beautiful temples for the Lord—or we should!

These elements of religion are important, but they are not the most important. If the vestments are too ornate and florid, they can sometimes draw attention to themselves. If everything in church was seen to be extravagantly expensive, it is natural for people to react in the other direction. So after the Second Vatican Council they went for what they regarded as relevant, up-to-date simplicity.

They replaced beautiful artwork with felt banners; they tore out beautiful altar pieces and plopped down shoddy wooden tables instead. They used pottery chalices and patens and bought cheap, lurid polyester vestments because they considered them suitably inexpensive and up-to-date. The beautiful old statues were put in the cellar. The vestments (which were probably worn out anyway) were burnt and the churches were stripped of beauty. Traditional Catholics are now reacting against this revolution, and I'm on their side.

However, there is such a thing as balance. If anything in the liturgy draws attention to itself, then it is excessive. Just as cheap, lurid vestments draw attention to themselves, so wildly extravagant Baroque vestments, hugely expensive sacred vessels and over-the-top liturgical parades may also draw attention to the outward signs more than to what they signify. If everything in the liturgy should complement and not distract from the action at the altar, then vestments, along with everything else, should be high-quality, traditional in design, and modest in their cost. They are there to enhance the worship, and their symbolic effect is all the stronger for being understated, discreet, and subordinate to the action of the Mass. An old manual on church art I once read stated: "the vestments should not attempt to preach except by the quality of the materials and the skill of the craftsmanship."

If you are in a position to purchase new vestments, don't fall for the latest fashion trend. For a time it was trendy to have wheat and grapes or a Holy Spirit dove embroidered on a chasuble. This draws attention to itself. Then for a time it was the fashion to have a strip of fine tapestry on the chasuble. That is now looking dated. If you are ordering vestments, be traditional because that has stood the test of time and will continue to do so. Gothic chasubles with simple orphreys and traditional embroidered designs are just fine. Fiddleback chasubles in a traditional style do the job. You can get these from some very fine and expensive suppliers, but you can also purchase perfectly adequate vestments online; if you have a seamstress in the parish you can get volunteers to make them—purchasing the fabrics and supplies from any of the church catalog suppliers.

The last thing I wanted to mention was the cassock. Should you wear the cassock when you're out and about? There are pros and cons. If you're wearing the cassock to show off or seem special, forget about it. However, sometimes the cassock, like the religious habit of the monks and nuns, helps to bear witness before the world.

I have to tell you about the time I was wearing my cassock and stopped for some Krispy Kreme donuts. I'm waiting in the line and (as usual) people strike up a conversation with me.

This plump lady behind me says, "Are you a Catholic priest?"

"Yes, ma'am."

"I'm Catholic, but I'm from New Jersey. I don't go to church anymore."

"Do any Catholics in New Jersey go to church?" I ask, joking.

"Very funny, Father. Where is your church?"

I tell her and invite her. The young guy in scrubs in front of me says, "My parents are both Lutherans."

"Where do you work?"

"The intensive care unit."

"Whoa! Me too. Spiritual intensive care."

He laughs.

"Are you Lutheran?"

"Yeah."

"I can help you with that…"

So when I step up to get my donuts the girl says, "That guy in scrubs paid for your donuts."

That's one of the great things about wearing the cassock. Nobody mistakes you for a Protestant pastor! People generally love to see priests in cassocks and religious in their habits. I encourage you to get into the habit habit. It opens doors and reminds people that there are some folks who are living their lives totally dedicated to God.

They say the red garments of the cardinals are meant to remind them that they may be called to shed their blood for the faith. I like that symbolism, and we can devise something similar with the cassock: when you wear the cassock, let the black color remind you of your faults and your need for the Lord's mercy, and then wear it confidently as a joyful witness!

14

Music: Praying Twice

D<small>EAR</small> M<small>ICHAEL</small>,

There is probably no subject in church life which arouses more attention and contention than the choice of music for Mass. In my travels around the country I have experienced every sort of music from Fauré to folk, from Palestrina to pop-rock, and from Elgar to gospel, and just about everything else you can imagine. Furthermore, if you read the chapter in Pope Benedict XVI's *The Spirit of the Liturgy* about church music you'll realize that church music has always been a contentious issue.

In every case there was a struggle between the sacred music of the church and the popular music of the age. In the United States today it is no different. In the majority of parishes a certain style of music has been adopted which can best be described as American folk-pop. With light, singable tunes and words that are often sentimental, this music reflects the style of popular secular music. It also illustrates perfectly what I was saying earlier about the shift of attention away from worship to fellowship and away from sacrifice toward sacred feast.

If you stop to analyze the words of popular Catholic songs, you soon realize that in these the people often sing about themselves, their gathering together, and the work they are called to do in the world. Other songs are highly sentimental and personal, and are more about one's feelings about God and spirituality than they are about the worship of God the Almighty Father.

I don't know if they give you much training in seminary on sacred music, but the basic principles are very important to think through. The simplest historical truth is that Jews and Christians sing. Other religions have had a kind of dull chanting that helps evoke a trance-like state, but they don't sing. The Jews sang the psalms and Christians, as St Paul teaches, should sing "psalms and hymns and spiritual songs." St Augustine said when we sing we "pray twice." In other words, we pray with the words and with the music.

Why is sacred music so important? Because music itself is a peculiar and mystical gift. We take it for granted—but have you ever pondered the mystery of music? Through the beauty of harmonious sound we share in the beauty of eternity. In the Middle Ages they believed that the planets moved in a harmonious way and that all the heavenly bodies moved in measure like music or like a dance, and the Scriptures tell us there is music in heaven—beautiful, awesome, tremble-inducing music. What would it be like if we could hear the music of the spheres and the singing of the planets on their way?

Sacred music in church is meant to bring us to the threshold of heaven—where we hear echoes of eternity. The music in church should therefore be otherworldly, transcendent, and sublime. I'm going to talk about the kind of music that accomplishes this best, but first I'd like to say a few words about hymns.

Hymns were sung in the early Church, but they really took off after the Protestant revolution. The Protestant faith was more individualistic and fellowship-centered, so congregational singing became a staple part of its worship. After the Second Vatican Council, as the emphasis shifted away from the sacrifice to the sacred feast and toward fellowship, it was natural for hymn-singing to become more popular among Catholics.

This is not necessarily a bad thing, but we should remember that hymns are not an authentic part of the Roman liturgy. At best they should be used as a complement to the music of the sacred liturgy. They should not replace it. The Mass should not turn into what some people call "a hymn sandwich"—bits of liturgy with lots of hymns stuck in here, there, and everywhere.

If you are unfamiliar with the hymns that are out there—get familiar. There are various websites where you can search for hymns, hear the tunes being played, and learn the hymns that are available. Also, there are more good resources for church music than ever before.

However, there is such a thing as a good hymn and a bad hymn, and no matter which way your tastes lie, you shouldn't fall into the trap of thinking that a hymn is good or bad simply because it is old or new. There are plenty of bad old hymns and good new hymns, just as there are good old hymns and bad new ones. A hymn can be judged on its own merits; it is not good or bad just because it is old or new.

Nonetheless, it is generally true that the older hymns are better—not because they're old, but because they have stood the test of time. The bad stuff falls away. For the most part, the good remains.

So what constitutes a good hymn? First of all, the words should be a poem of praise to God—not a description of the good works we want to do in the world. You should ask whether the hymn gives glory and praise to God. Next we ask whether the words convey orthodox Catholic theology. A good hymn teaches the faith as well as lifts the heart to God. Third, we ask whether the words are good poetry. If the rhymes are trite, the symbols clichéd, the sentiment sickly, or the imagery shallow and poor, then the hymn is unworthy.

As I've said, the Catholic Church has not had a tradition of good hymns. The Protestant tradition has a much richer treasury of hymns, and that is not a bad thing. Many of the classic hymns from the Anglican and Lutheran tradition are perfectly fine doctrinally, and when you look at their history you'll find that a good number of the hymns from the Anglican tradition are hymns from the ancient Church that have been translated into English. This is one of the gifts of the Anglo-Catholic movement in the Church.

The other significant feature of the hymn is the music. A congregational hymn should have a regular rhythm and be easy for the congregation to learn and sing.

Finally, there are different types of hymns for different

points in the liturgy. A processional hymn should be a solid, singable hymn of praise to God. If it can connect with the readings of the day and the theme of worship, all the better. A hymn during or after communion should be quieter and more reverent. This is also the place to use some of the more personal and devotional hymns. If there is a recessional, that is the place for hymns like *Forth in Thy Name, O Lord, We Go* that encourage the faithful in their work in the world.

I began by talking about hymns, but to be honest, hymns should play, at most, a secondary role in the music for the liturgy. *Sacrosanctum Concilium*—the Second Vatican Council's document on the liturgy—says that Gregorian chant and sacred polyphony are the forms of music that should be used for the liturgy. Hymns—sung by the choir—should only be used to complement the proper music of the liturgy.

You are probably familiar with Gregorian chant. Sacred polyphony is different from most of the music we are used to because instead of there being a melody line around which harmonies are woven, there are several voice parts all singing their own lines, which are woven together for a uniquely sacred and Catholic sound.

There are several good reasons for promoting Gregorian chant and sacred polyphony. Firstly, once people get used to it, they love it. These two forms of music have an especially reverent and spiritual "feel" to them. Instead of adopting the musical styles of the secular world in an attempt to be relevant, Gregorian chant and sacred polyphony have a sound all their own. It is a sound that is sublime, transcendental, and distinctively Catholic.

Furthermore, Gregorian chant is surprisingly easy for choirs to learn and eventually master. There is a simplicity to chant that means it can be performed by a small choir or a large group. There is also an amazing amount of flexibility. Gregorian chant can be adapted for men's or women's voices—adults or children or a mixture of all of them.

But there is another reason why I think Gregorian chant and sacred polyphony are making a comeback. It is because we are moving away from cultural Catholicism. What do I mean by this? Well, so much of the Catholic religion around the world was, in the past, linked with particular cultures. We had Irish Catholicism and Polish Catholicism, Italian and Portuguese and English and French Catholicism. Each ethnic or cultural group had its own culture, its own customs, and its own music.

But cultural Catholicism is breaking down. The customs associated with a particular ethnicity don't continue into a second or third generation. With increased global mobility, the ethnic and cultural barriers are disintegrating. Increasingly our local churches reflect the diversity of a global church. Nigerians and Vietnamese worshipping in an American church will not easily connect with the vestiges of Irish, Polish, or Italian Catholicism that came to America with our great-grandparents. Likewise, American Catholics won't connect with African or Latin American music and customs.

What *does* connect with all Catholics and transcends culture is the timeless liturgy of the Church and the timeless sacred music of the Catholic tradition. Gregorian chant and sacred polyphony are not exclusively Italian or French, English or Spanish. They are just Catholic, and as such represent a treasure that should be shared by Catholics of every culture, ethnicity, and language. Because this music transcends time, place, and culture it is a force for unity in Catholic worship.

Those who argue for music that is up-to-date and "relevant" will say Gregorian chant and sacred polyphony are boring, dull, or gloomy. It has to be admitted that when these are sung poorly they do sound pretty bad! However, let's face it: any kind of music performed badly is awful. The answer to poorly sung Gregorian chant is not to ban Gregorian chant, but to work harder to sing it well.

To introduce this music to an American parish is not always easy. First, there has to be a general shift from the contemporary hymns toward the sacred tradition. To do this you will need to hire the right music director, someone sympathetic and knowledgeable, and you will need to pay him or her at the appropriate level!

You also need to move slowly as your musicians and parishioners get used to what may seem to them a new form of music. In addition, this music cannot stand alone. You will need to ensure that all the other parts of the liturgy are also reverent and inspiring so that the music complements the solemn celebration of Mass and does not distract from it.

As the component parts of the liturgy begin to come together you will experience (and you will witness your people experiencing) a subtle and profound reorientation of their worship. The sacred music will combine with the more solemn celebration of the liturgy to bring about a more contemplative, reverent, and transcendent attitude and atmosphere.

Without even being completely conscious of it, you and your people's hearts will be lifted to the Lord. Your attention will turn away from yourselves and toward Him. Your energy and focus will be directed primarily toward worship and secondarily toward your work in the world—and that is as it should be, for Our Lord said, "The first and greatest commandment is to love the Lord your God. The second is like it—love your neighbor as yourself" (Mt. 22:38–39). The second commandment actually depends on the first. Loving your neighbor, on its own, is just being a good neighbor, but loving your neighbor as the result of loving God first means you see Christ in your neighbor, and that transforms everything.

A transformation in music is therefore part of the reorientation of the worship from being people-centered to being God-centered. Finally, remember what I wrote about the sub-linguistic and supra-linguistic aspects of worship? Music is vital because it communicates with words, but also the music itself is a form of communication that is above words. Like art, which is visual, music speaks a language which is not verbal. This is where Gregorian chant in Latin has a place. We should remember that *Sacrosanctum Concilium* instructs, "The Church acknowledges Gregorian chant as specially suited to the Roman liturgy: therefore, other things being equal, it should be given pride of place in liturgical services" (SC, 116).

A translation of the words should be provided, but even if the people do not follow the translation, the Gregorian chant in words they do not understand can, on its own, transport them to a more contemplative and spiritual plane.

It is difficult to explain exactly what I mean because the whole subject is beyond language. So let me give you an example. In my car I listen to Italian opera. I was driving along with my son Elias the other day and switched on Puccini's *La Bohème*. Elias said, "Is it better because it's in Italian?"

"Yes," I replied. "Because the words and the music fit together perfectly. They were written for each other. But there is more to it than that."

"Okay? But you don't know what they're singing."

"Yes, but I do because I know Rodolpho and Mimi are starving artists and they have just met and are enchanted with one another and are falling in love. I know the opera well enough to know that is what is going on in the scene."

"So?"

"Well, I don't need to know exactly what they are singing to each other word for word, and because I don't know the exact meaning of all the words I can sense and feel the emotion of the scene much more."

"So by not knowing the meaning of the words you know the feeling of the words."

"That's right. The literal, verbal mind is switched off and the non-verbal heart is opened . . . which is what opera is all about."

I think the same applies to the liturgy. How do you open the heart—so often locked against the mystery, beauty, and love of God? Maybe it is through music with words you do not always understand.

This is also the value of a pipe organ. Halfway through building our new church my deacon said, "Father, what are we going to do about the organ? We need a pipe organ." By this time I was exasperated and exhausted with the fundraising effort. We hadn't budgeted anything for any organ at all, not even an electronic squeak box of an organ—the kind with illuminated keys and a rumba beat. My deacon said if we were going to build this church we should do it right. I said (like many pastors), "We'll add the organ later."

Deacon replied, "Then it will never be done."

I knew he was right, but I also knew that a pipe organ would be expensive, so I said, "Tell you what, deacon. I'm tired of asking people for money. Why don't you raise the money for the pipe organ?"

So he did. He got together with the financial team and we found a way to purchase and install a salvaged pipe organ, and we're so glad we did. It adds depth, beauty, and a transcendent quality to our worship, just like it says in *Sacrosanctum Concilium*... "In the Latin Church the pipe organ is to be held in high esteem, for it is the traditional musical instrument which adds a wonderful splendor to the Church's ceremonies and powerfully lifts up man's mind to God and to higher things" (SC 120).

The pure music of the pipe organ penetrates our ears and takes us to the doorway to another world. The sonorous tones of a pipe organ resonate in our hearts in a way beyond words, and the sustained sound can accompany hymns or chant in a way no other instrument can. Likewise, the beautiful Gregorian chant and sacred polyphony echo in our hearts and minds and lift us beyond this ordinary, literal, practical world to the very threshold of heaven.

15

Redeeming the Time

DEAR MICHAEL,

Did I say that for my vacation last summer I took a trip to England and made my retreat at Quarr Abbey? Quarr was built in the first years of the twentieth century when the monks from the Abbey of Solesmes were expelled from France along with the other Catholic religious.

They came to the Isle of Wight—an island about fourteen miles wide just off the southern coast of England. At that point the monks had to plan for the eventuality that they would never return to France. One member of the community, Dom Paul Bellot, was an amazingly creative architect, and in a very short time they built the beautiful and unique monastery buildings. You should visit sometime. It's a fantastic place!

I first visited Quarr when I was a young Anglican priest, and I was immediately captivated. I remember during one visit coming out of the abbey church to see an English teenager leaning against a tree smoking a cigarette. He was all decked out in gothic gear: black jeans and T-shirt, black leather jacket, big black boots, and dyed black spiky hair. He had tattoos, heavy eye makeup—the works. So I stopped to speak to him. He looked me up and down suspiciously.

"What are you looking at?"

"Just eyeing up your outfit," I said. "Seeing how some-body else does black."

He gave me a sly grin.

"Why are you here anyway?" I asked.

He paused for a minute, then said, "Because this is where the power is. Right?"

"Yeah," I nodded, "You're right. This is where the power is."

I've found that to be the case every time I've returned to Quarr. There is a magic about the place that makes it like a little Narnia. The veil between this world and the next is very thin at Quarr.

One of the most striking things about a visit to Quarr is the slow pace. To start with, the Isle of Wight itself is cut off from the hurried pace of the rest of England, and the pace of life on the island always does seem a bit slower. That's not the only thing, however. The monks themselves cultivate a slower pace of life. The WiFi is only turned on for eight hours a day. They don't have a car or television. They keep a monastic schedule that is traditional—with seven offices of worship each day. The food is simple and the life austere.

I'm spending some time talking about Quarr in order to evoke an atmosphere—so you might imagine what it is like to live and work in a monastery where the whole day and the whole life is given to the worship of God. At Quarr—like the other Benedictine monasteries of the Solesmes congregation—the liturgy is the heart of their life. They focus on Gregorian chant and dedicate their lives to the liturgy.

This means they live at a slower pace—God's pace. I want to speak to you about redeeming the time in the liturgy and the liturgical year, but first I want you to get a glimpse of why this is important. I think it is important to get used to God's slow pace because God, as the master of time, has lots of time. God never hurries. Sometimes in parish life, when people are worried about their loved ones who have left the faith, or they want to accomplish something for God and things are just not moving as quickly as they'd like, I'll say, "Slow down. We can slow down. God plays a long game."

I've seen this in my life and in the lives of my family and people I've worked with. Sometimes the reconciliation, forgiveness, and peace only come after a long, hard struggle. The timing has to be right. Sometimes, only at the end of life do we find the God and the love for which we have been searching our whole lives.

The same is true in the history of the world's redemption. God starts small and builds slowly. He began his work with one man—a wandering nomad in Mesopotamia and Arabia whose name was Abraham. From there, through many centuries God did his slow, methodical work in the world until finally, a girl was born without sin who would reverse Eve's rebellion and bear God into the world. Now he still moves slowly and plays the long game. Humanity and the whole world are redeemed, but he's still bringing the whole drama to its final act. He's the

Alpha and the Omega—the Lord of Time. Time is his, and he moves slowly.

This is why the monks at Quarr move slowly. They move slowly around the monastery and they move slowly around the church. They move slowly in the liturgy, in a dignified and stately way, because they are marching to the quiet, steady drumbeat of the Lord.

Therefore, one of the simple principles of moving in church, and especially in the sanctuary, is to move slowly and deliberately. Teach the altar servers this too. They should not run in church, and when setting up for Mass they should move slowly. People are watching them; their reverent, dignified service is a beautiful thing to see, and it aids prayer and worship.

During the liturgy itself all should move deliberately and naturally—always confident in where they are going and what they are doing. We can add a grace and dignity to the liturgy simply through body language.

In Benedictine monasteries, the monks follow St Benedict's rule of greeting one another with a bow. This little ceremony should be part of the liturgy and the interaction between clergy and servers. The little bow of gratitude and acknowledgment adds a ceremonial feel to the liturgy that takes everyone into the realm of symbol and ritual rather than everyday behavior and gestures. This also sets up the proper way for the faithful to share the kiss of peace: it is a liturgical action done with solemnity and simplicity. It should not be a happy wave with a "Hey! How are you guys! Where are you going for brunch after Mass?"

The slowness of God's pace brings me to the other aspect of redeeming the time: the Divine Office. The daily cycle of prayer is a chance in the midst of our busy and crowded life to slow down to God's pace. This works beautifully in the monastery: the bells ring, the monks make their way to the church, and the office is sung. This is the reason of their life and the reason of their vocation, and because the time is set and the expectation is there it is easier to fulfill the obligation.

If we are in the world, this vital aspect of the liturgical life becomes more difficult. We're busy. There is so much to do. There are so many people who demand our time. Life is fast-paced and we want to get things done. To stop for the Divine Office means we have to put on the brakes, slow down, and stop. Even if you do take the time for Divine Office, if you're like me, you often race through it, taking short cuts and not paying close enough attention. Maybe you don't bother at all—not because you don't love God, but because you're caught up in the hectic pace of life.

I can't stress enough that it is through the routine of the Divine Office that God does great things in our life. When we slow down to his pace we can more easily walk with him. Slowing down also means being quiet—and how can we listen to the still, small voice of the Lord if our heads are full of noise and our hearts and minds are busy with many thoughts and emotions? The greatest thing about reciting the Divine Office is not necessarily all the words of the psalms and prayers, but the time that is spent with God at his pace and in his place.

Finally, the monks at Quarr reminded me again of the importance of God's time because God's time is linked with God's timing. God's work in the world comes to fruition when it is ready—when everything comes together and all the pieces that seemed a confused jumble suddenly fit, and we can see the hand of providence at work. The more we become aware of God's timing, the more we become aware of His intricate work of grace throughout human history.

My Sunday school teacher used to say, "History is His Story." The modernists and relativists would have us believe that there is no overarching meaning of history—that history is a series of unrelated, random events and what we do is impose a meaning and order on these events as a child lying on the hillside on a summer day might look into the clouds and see an elephant, a camel, or a giant ogre riding a motorcycle.

There is a little bit of Catholic genius we take for granted that turns upside-down the idea that history is a random collection of events. That secret is the liturgical year. First, the liturgical year, as you know, is structured around the two hinges of Christmas and Easter. Everything revolves around Holy Week and the annual commemoration of Christ's Passion, Death and Resurrection. That is the center of time, the heart of history, and the axis upon which the world turns. Advent and Christmas are the lead-up to Lent and the Paschal feast.

This annual cycle is a constant reminder that history has meaning and that there is one event around which the whole world turns. The Paschal mystery transcends time and fills time with its meaning. Stop for a moment to consider: here is an event that took place two thousand years ago in the Roman Empire—but through the liturgical cycles we see how, for two thousand years before, the world was anticipating and looking forward to that event, and two thousand years later the human race is still pondering that event, remembering that event, or rebelling against that event.

Through the gentle rhythm of the liturgical year—harmonizing as it does with the seasons of darkness and light, springtime and harvest—the very cycles of the earth, moon, stars, and sky connect like cogs in a cosmic machine to pound home the truth that God is moving as the creative Spirit within and through the triumphs and tragedies of human history.

The celebrations of the saints within this cycle bring home the point that God does this work in every age through the lives of ordinary men and women. Down through history fishermen and tent-makers, soldiers and slaves, queens and scholars, old men and maidens, mystics and martyrs have found the Lord and followed the sign of the cross unto their final destiny. Each year as we remember them over and again (and then see new saints and blesseds raised to the altar) we are reminded that God is not working his purpose out through grandiose schemes, five-year plans, or philosophical schools of thought. He is not completing his plan through economic theories, political stratagems, or the marching of emperors' armies.

He is accomplishing his plan through the lives of little ones. He is working out this cosmic plan in a hidden corner of the world through a shepherd girl or a missionary monk tramping across the Alps. He is using a science teacher who decides to work with the poor, or a bishop who stands up against tyranny only to be gunned down while saying Mass for some nuns. He is using a scholar who ate too much pickled herring or a simpleton who could levitate and fly. Here he used a simple French parish priest; there he used the Lord Chancellor of England.

The liturgical year, therefore, is a great and wonderful encyclopedia of grace. It is a compendium of providence and a daily reminder that God has been at work in the world from Eden onward, and that He is not done with us yet.

Select Bibliography

Beauduin, Lambert. *Liturgy: The Life of the Church*. College-ville, MN: Liturgical Press, 1926.

Caronti, Emmanuele. *The Spirit of the Liturgy*. Collegeville, MN: Liturgical Press, 1926.

Dix, Gregory. *The Shape of the Liturgy*. London: Adam and Charles Black, 1984.

Guardini, Romano. *The Spirit of the Liturgy*. Trans. Ada Lane. London: Sheed and Ward, 1937.

Hani, Jean. *The Divine Liturgy: Insights into Its Mystery*. Kettering, OH: Angelico Press, 2008.

Jones, Cheslyn, Geoffrey Wainwright, and Edward Yarnold, eds. *The Study of Liturgy*. London: SPCK, 1978.

Lang, Uwe Michael. *Turning Toward the Lord*. San Francisco: Ignatius Press, 2004.

Mosebach, Martin. *The Heresy of Formlessness*. Trans. Graham Harrison. Brooklyn, NY: Angelico Press, 2018.

Ratzinger, Joseph. *The Spirit of the Liturgy*. San Francisco: Ignatius Press, 2000.

Reid, Alcuin, ed. *Liturgy in the Twenty-First Century*. London: T&T Clark, 2016.

Reid, Alcuin, ed. *Sacred Liturgy*. San Francisco: Ignatius Press, 2014.

About the Author

FR. DWIGHT LONGENECKER was raised in an Evangelical home and was ordained as a priest in the Church of England. In 2006 he and his family returned to his native USA where he was ordained as a Catholic priest under the Pastoral Provision for married convert clergy. He is author of over twenty books, a blogger, podcaster, and popular speaker nationwide, and serves as Pastor of Our Lady of the Rosary Church in Greenville, South Carolina.

CPSIA information can be obtained
at www.ICGtesting.com
Printed in the USA
FSHW011722070320
67788FS